C000180569

ALAIN PROST

By NIGEL ROEBUCK

HAZLETON PUBLISHING

PUBLISHER
Richard Poulter

EXECUTIVE PUBLISHER
Elizabeth Le Breton

ART EDITOR
Steve Small

PRODUCTION MANAGER
George Greenfield

PRODUCTION CONTROLLER
Peter Lovering

PRODUCTION ASSISTANT
Deirdre Fenney

STATISTICS
John Taylor

The colour photographs appearing on the front and back covers
and pages 65–80 are by Keith Sutton.

Black and white photographs contributed by:
Keith Sutton, Nigel Snowdon, Diana Burnett, International
Press Agency, Marlboro, Peter McFadyen and Tim Tyler.

This first edition published in 1990 by
Hazleton Publishing, 3 Richmond Hill, Richmond,
Surrey TW10 6RE.

ISBN: 0-905138-69-4

Printed in England by BAS Printers Ltd, Over Wallop,
Hampshire.

Typesetting by First Impression Graphics Ltd, Richmond,
Surrey.

© Hazleton Securities Ltd, 1990. No part of this publication
may be reproduced, or transmitted, in any form or by any
means, electronic, mechanical, photocopying, recording or
otherwise, without prior permission in writing from Hazleton
Securities Ltd.

DISTRIBUTORS

UK & OTHER MARKETS
Osprey Publishing Limited, 59 Grosvenor Street
London W1X 9DA

NORTH AMERICA
Motorbooks International, PO Box 2
729 Prospect Avenue, Osceola
Wisconsin 54020, USA

Paul Oxman Publishing, 17165 Newhope
Unit M, Fountain Valley, CA 92708, USA

AUSTRALIA
Technical Book & Magazine Co. Pty
289-299 Swanston Street
Melbourne, Victoria 3000

Universal Motor Publications
c/o Automoto Motoring Bookshop
152-154 Clarence Street
Sydney 2000, New South Wales

NEW ZEALAND
David Bateman Limited, PO Box 65062
Mairangi Bay, Auckland 10

'See you at Elf for lunch, OK?' This, apart from 'Who's quickest?', is about the only question every journalist can be guaranteed to ask at every Grand Prix. Over time the Elf motorhome has been a sanctuary for the press, a place for sustenance, a glass of wine or two, a chat.

Once in a while, too, a driver drops by, invariably one sponsored by the French petroleum company. He knocks on the door, and pays his respects to François Guiter, the long-time competitions boss – and a man, probably, responsible for the lift-off of more Formula 1 careers than any other individual.

There is a steeliness about Guiter, but also a lovely, quiet and dry humour. He knows Formula 1. One afternoon, late in 1979, he introduced me to a shy young fellow who had unobtrusively hung around the motorhome for a while, on and off. 'This', he said, 'is Alain Prost.'

Earlier that year we had watched Prost dominate the Formula 3 race at Monte Carlo, but perhaps it had made less impression than it should: that race is nearly always won by a French up-and-comer, and quite often his career makes little progress thereafter.

Once Prost had left, I mentioned this to Guiter. 'Yes, yes, I know,' he agreed, 'but this one...this one is different. This one will be great.' And a French journalist friend, who had seen a lot of Alain's races, concurred. Prost, he had a feeling, would emerge as the best driver his country had ever produced.

At Monza Alain was back again, still looking a little lost and forlorn. By now he had clinched the European F3 Championship: how were things looking for 1980? I asked. 'Mmmm, not so good. I have no money for a season of F2 next year. That's why I started coming to Grands Prix, hoping there might be something here.'

And had anything turned up? 'Well, my best chance seems to be Ligier, but they want money, and I don't think they really want a young driver. And I've spoken to Brabham and Lotus, but...'

At that point McLaren was not in his thoughts, but Fred Opert, for whom Prost had driven a couple of F2 races, had been impressed, and spoke highly of him to Marlboro. From nowhere, Alain was offered a drive in the last race of the year, at Watkins Glen. And Teddy Mayer has probably never got over the fact that Prost turned him down.

This is not mainstream behaviour for an aspiring Formula 1 driver. Many a star over the years has got on his way in machinery which would later make him shudder: you say yes immediately, worry about the consequences later. Not Prost – despite the fact that his offer came from a leading team. Already, he was looking like a man apart.

Below: *Donington, May 1979. Prost leads Johansson and Placido Iglesias. In 1987 Alain and Stefan would be team-mates at McLaren.*

Right: *Alain, here leading at Zandvoort, dominated the European Formula 3 Championship with his Martini-Renault in 1979. Nevertheless, he had no clear view of his future until the McLaren offer came up for 1980. At Donington (above) he suffered a rare defeat.*

Inset: *Prost's early showings in the McLaren rather demoralised John Watson, then going through a bad spell. To the newcomer's embarrassment, members of the team were not slow to point it out.* Main picture: *Alain follows John at Interlagos, the scene of his second F1 race, in which he finished fifth.*

'In fact, it was one of my best decisions,' he thinks. 'They already had two cars entered, for Watson and Tambay, and I had never even driven a Formula 1 car. I told them the agreement would be bad for them, bad for me. Instead I asked them to let me have a test at Paul Ricard, and I went there with Watson and Kevin Cogan, who was also being considered by the team. It was a very nice test, and I was quicker than both of them.'

Immediately Mayer signed Prost for 1980, as team-mate to Watson, and the season began after the fashion of the test, with the novice outpacing the number one. At the time John was suffering from a major loss of confidence, and Alain became slightly embarrassed by the very obvious way Mayer increasingly regarded him as team leader.

'I was surprised to be quicker than Watson,' Prost recalls, 'but he wasn't driving then as he could drive – and *did* drive later. It was a difficult time to be at McLaren, but more so for him. The cars weren't very competitive, for sure. OK, a young guy will push harder in that situation, but it was difficult for John, who had been in Formula 1 for years.'

Alain was exceptional from the start, sixth in his first Grand Prix, fifth in his second. But after South America came Kyalami; and here the worries began. Prost had two accidents in two days – and each was the consequence of a suspension failure. The first one didn't hurt him, but in the second he broke a wrist, which meant missing Long Beach.

'That car, the M29, was always breaking. Over the season I had six or seven serious accidents. You know, if your car loses a wheel in every race, I think it's not good,' he says, with delightful understatement. 'And I don't think any driver can accept that. The worst was at the end of the year, in qualifying at Watkins Glen, where the suspension broke in a fourth-gear corner. I hit the wall very hard, and got a big bang on the head. That was something, I can tell you – I was knocked out.

'When I got back to the pits eventually, I heard people in the team telling journalists I had made a mistake, gone too fast on cold tyres – and already I'd done eight laps! The following day they wanted me to race, even though I knew after the warm-up I wasn't fit. My head ached like hell, and I hadn't been able to sleep all night.

'After their remarks to the press after the accident, I made up my mind to leave. I said, "OK, if you want to say things like that, it's finished. I have a three-year contract with you, but I won't drive for you any more. If you won't release me, OK, I stop Formula 1."'

At the time there was a lot of bitterness within McLaren, some of whose personnel

Above left: *Zolder 1980. Already Prost
knew the McLaren M29 was neither
competitive nor especially trustworthy, but he
always impressed with the car. At Brands
Hatch (left) Alain qualified a second faster
than team-mate Watson, and finished sixth
with the recalcitrant M29. Above: French
triumvirate. In the British Grand Prix the
Ligiers, driven by Didier Pironi (left) and
Jacques Laffite (right) were the class of the
field. Alain, the new boy, listens respectfully.
At Monaco (top) Prost was one of several
drivers eliminated in a first-corner accident
when Derek Daly went skyward with his
Tyrrell after forgetting to brake…*

claimed they had given Prost his first chance in Formula 1, only to see him now being 'poached' by Renault, who had lost no time in signing him. At the time Alain defended himself vigorously.

'When I sign a contract, I mean it. When I give my word, I mean it. Whatever people say, I did *not* leave McLaren because I received a better offer. After Montreal, with one race left, I didn't know what to do: I felt I should stay with McLaren, because of my contract with them, but at the same time I was getting more and more worried about suspension failures all the time – you reach a point where you *expect* the car to break, where you are waiting for it to happen! And in those circumstances you can't drive properly. But what happened at the Glen really made up my mind for me.'

Had Prost been willing to break his contract for the sake of convenience, he added, he would have done it some little time before. By March 1980 – only two races into his Grand Prix career – he had been contacted by Ferrari's Marco Piccinini: would Alain partner Gilles Villeneuve in the team for 1981?

'Like anyone else, I had always wanted to drive for Ferrari, but I wasn't prepared to break my McLaren contract. By the time I made up my mind to leave, at Watkins Glen, Didier Pironi had already signed.'

Although it did not end as he might have wished, Alain's first year in Formula 1 had been remarkably impressive. He says he often dreamed of life as a Grand Prix driver, but rarely saw it as more than that: a dream.

Like many of his contemporaries, he began with karts. 'In the early Seventies I raced against Patrese, de Angelis, Cheever, Teo Fabi – even Arnoux. And it started as fun, nothing more. In fact, I only began to think seriously about being a racing driver when I won one or two important things...the French Championship, the European Junior Championship. Then I won the FFSA scholarship to go to racing drivers' school, won the Pilote Elf competition and some money for Formule Renault.'

Hence the reverence for M. Guiter.

'It was at that point I decided I wanted to go all the way. I'd worked in my father's furniture factory for a year, but then I had to do my military service – at the same time as going to the racing school and the European Kart Championship. That could have been difficult for me.'

So how had he contrived to negotiate time off for these non-military matters?

A sheepish grin. 'Well, I was the how-you-say secretary of the captain. I had to sign all the applications for leave so...I just signed for myself as well! It was the only way.'

In 1976, free of the army now, Alain dominated Formule Renault, and the following

Pages 18-19: The one-off McLaren M30
made its debut at Zandvoort in 1980. It was a
little more competitive than the M29, but still
Prost needed to drive hard for sixth place.

year Formule Renault Europe. There was a brief glitch in the irresistible rise in 1978, his first season in Formula 3, because Renault's new engine was off the pace. But in 1979 there was almost unbroken success: Prost's Martini-Renault took the European Championship, and walked away with the prestigious race in Monte Carlo.

The Renault link was already well established, therefore, when he joined the Formula 1 team for 1981. And although there was nothing to that effect in his contract, Alain went there on the tacit understanding – agreed between Competitions Director Gérard Larrousse and himself – that it was as number two to René Arnoux, already a Renault driver for two seasons. And at first all seemed to be well between the two, although Prost faced the same problem as at McLaren the previous year: immediately he was quicker than his supposed team leader, who suffered a huge loss of confidence, reflected in his driving.

Prost's first win came, appropriately, at Dijon that summer, but amid some controversy. Thanks to the intervention of a brief shower of monsoon proportions, the French Grand Prix was a two-part affair, and *après le déluge* soft Michelins were the thing to have. Alain had them. Most people's sympathy, though, was with Nelson Piquet, a convincing leader until the cloudburst.

There could be no argument, though, about his second victory, which was scored at Zandvoort after a tough battle with the Williams of Alan Jones. It was the first public Formula 1 exhibition of Prost the thinker.

'I decided exactly how I was going to run it, and it went exactly to plan. Very satisfying. Alan overtook me briefly towards the end of a lap, and I passed him again immediately – I knew I had to do that. When he was behind me, he was upset to be there, and he screwed his tyres – which I wanted him to do. If I had been behind, for sure I would have screwed *my* tyres. As it was, they were destroyed by the end of the race. If Alan and I had fought all through the race, neither of us would have finished.'

Two weeks later there was a flag-to-flag victory at Monza, and Prost ended the year with a superb second at Las Vegas, not at all Renault country at that stage of turbo engine development.

Arnoux, by contrast, had made little impression all year long, and for 1982 there was no argument about status. Officially Renault had no number one driver, and certainly René retained parity of equipment with Alain, but Prost was now obviously the man

Above left: *New year, new team, new overalls. For 1981 Prost joined Arnoux at Renault, and quickly asserted himself over René.* Left: *Buenos Aires 1981: Alain's third race for Renault – and first points for the team. In the RE20 he finished third, behind Piquet and Reutemann.*

*Monaco 1981. The Renaults were way off the
pace at Monte Carlo, Prost working hard
(left) to qualify in the top ten. In the race
(above) he led team-mate Arnoux, but
neither finished – the more embarrassing on
home soil when a turbocharged Ferrari, driven
by Villeneuve, won the race. Alain was
becoming a little concerned.*

Alain's first Grand Prix victory, at Dijon in 1981, was a fortunate one, aided by a sudden rain storm. Above left: Prost leads erstwhile team-mate John Watson. Left: On the rostrum Alain celebrates, and Watson (right) is satisfied with second place. Piquet (left) is unhappy with third... Prost's second win, at Zandvoort (above), was a clear-cut affair, in which he beat Alan Jones. Top: The third win, easy this time, came at Monza.

Right: *After winning the opening race of 1982, at Kyalami, Prost was also victorious at Rio – but only after Piquet and Rosberg had been disqualified.*

to whom the Régie looked for its success. The irony was that in 1982 Arnoux rediscovered all his old pace...

It was, in Prost's words, 'a shitty year – a season I hated, when everything possible seemed to go wrong', but it began well enough for him, with victory in the first two races.

There was trauma everywhere in Formula 1 at that time. FISA, having tried unsuccessfully to reduce downforce by banning skirts, capitulated for 1982: skirts were back, albeit fixed rather than sliding. And this, of course, obliged teams to run their cars with truck springs, so as to keep the skirts from destroying themselves on the track surface. There was no suspension movement worth the name, so that the cars were hideously uncomfortable to drive, their handling as progressive as a Starfighter.

As well as that, there remained a well of resentment – a legacy of the 'FISA/FOCA war' – between the 'grandee' teams (forging ahead with turbocharged engines) and Bernie Ecclestone's FOCA members, which continued to rely on the venerable normally aspirated Cosworth. Hence in early 1982 we had the 'water tank' phenomenon, which permitted the Cosworth brigade to race at well under the minimum weight limit. In Brazil Piquet's Brabham won, with Rosberg's Williams second and Prost's Renault third, but later the British cars were disqualified, elevating the French one to nine points. It was for this reason that the FOCA teams later boycotted the San Marino Grand Prix.

Even before Rio, however, there had been dissension of another kind. At Kyalami, scene of the opening race, the drivers went on strike, this in protest against the terms of a new 'superlicence' which FISA was attempting to foist upon them. The first day of qualifying went by the board, after which compromise was reached, and the race went ahead.

In the high altitude of the Transvaal the turbos had the race to themselves, and Prost was a class above the rest. After the Ferraris had retired, he had only Arnoux to concern him, and not even a puncture, and consequent pit stop, could keep him from winning easily. Nine points, and nine more would follow from Brazil.

Astonishingly, though, those two victories would be Alain's lot for 1982, a year in which no driver won more than two races, and in which the World Champion – Rosberg – won but one. Renault's lack of reliability was almost unrelenting. At Monaco Prost crashed out of the lead when the car broke with three laps to go, and engine-related problems put him out half a dozen times: in Austria when he was leading with ease, five laps from the end.

Alain looked set for victory at Monte Carlo (right), *leading most of the way in the RE30B. But with a couple of laps to go, the car broke, pitching him into the guard rail.*

Controversy at Paul Ricard. Left: *The
Renault pit hangs out a board, reminding
Arnoux of his undertaking...* Below left:
*René wanted nothing of that, and kept ahead
of Prost throughout.* Bottom left: *The
Renault mechanics greet second-placed Prost
with enthusiasm – but that wasn't what Alain
was feeling...*

By his own admission, though, Alain was not at his best for much of the season. He was devastated at Zolder by the death of Villeneuve, a close friend, and at Hockenheim was involved in the accident which ended the career of Didier Pironi. In heavy rain the unsighted Ferrari driver hit the back of Prost's Renault, which was slowing to come into the pits. The day would have a lasting effect on Alain's attitude to racing in the rain: 'His car flew over the top of mine; and what I can't forget is that he hit me only because he couldn't *see* me.... What does that have to do with skill?'

And then there was Ricard, inevitably the most important race of Renault's season. Arnoux took the pole, with Prost beside him, but at this stage of the year René had only four points, and therefore not a prayer of the championship. Accordingly, Larrousse asked him to let Prost win, and he agreed.

'I was amazed he did that,' Alain says, 'because there's no way I would have done the same. But he did, and I believed him.'

After the Brabham-BMWs had accounted for themselves, the Renaults were home free. Arnoux led, but Prost was unconcerned – until René ignored a pit signal reminding him of his promise. Too late, Alain – and those in the Renault pit – realised that Arnoux was not about to cede his position: 'Afterwards I made my feelings clear, although I realise that's not always the smart thing to do.'

France, broadly, took Arnoux's side, with Prost depicted as the villain of the piece, the spoiled star who whinged because he hadn't been allowed to win, but had been beaten by this awkward and unsophisticated working-class boy from Grenoble.

That evening, driving home to Saint Chamond, Alain stopped for gas. 'You did the right thing, M. Arnoux,' said the pump attendant. 'Prost thinks everything should be handed to him on a plate.' The man knew little enough of racing to mix up the faces of the two drivers, but his prejudices were finely honed. Alain, embarrassed and furious, paid in cash rather than offer a credit card bearing his name.

'For a few days after that race, I decided absolutely to retire from Formula 1 at the end of the year. I couldn't believe the bad publicity I got,' he remembers, 'and I told Larrousse I would leave Renault if Arnoux stayed. In Formula 1 it's important to feel that everyone in the team is on the same side. Otherwise, it's not possible to drive well – not for me, anyway. You must trust your team-mate. I remembered what happened with Villeneuve, after Pironi duped him at Imola, and I learned a lesson from that – which later came back to me again in 1989, with Senna...'

Above: *At Dijon Alain chats with Niki Lauda, who made his Formula 1 comeback that year with great success. Two years later the two would be team-mates at McLaren.*

Below: *By the end of the 1982 season, Alain was getting bored with Renault's chronic unreliability. After taking the pole at Las Vegas (right), Prost tailed team-mate Arnoux in the early stages. He then led impressively, but late brake problems dropped him back to fourth.* Below right: *Late in the year Prost made his first visit to a country he would come to love, dominating the Formula Pacific Australian Grand Prix in a Ralt.*

Ayrton, though, was a future blight on his life. In the early Eighties Prost's only problem was with Arnoux. 'After Ricard he went on to the French press about how nothing had gone right for him, that he was always unlucky – the underdog. A martyr, you see, and the French adore martyrs. He had absolutely no reason to behave like one, but some of the journalists wrote that he had done the right thing. They didn't know the facts.'

It was the start of a running battle between Prost and the French press. With some of them he gets along fine – indeed, a handful are among his closest friends; but for many he has nothing but contempt, and the roots are there in the Renault days, when he was driving *pour la France*.

Below: *The Renault RE40 made its debut at
Long Beach in 1983, Prost finishing an
inauspicious 11th after sundry problems.*
Right: *Alain with Renault's Competitions
Director, Gérard Larrousse.* Below right:
*At Ricard, in April, there was success – a first
win for the RE40.*

Arnoux duly left the team at the end of the year, for Ferrari, and Eddie Cheever took over as Prost's team-mate for 1983. Yet again, it was a season in which Alain *should* have won the World Championship, for that year's car, the RE40, was one he loved, and one in which he won four races – more than Piquet, the man who eventually took the title.

Overleaf: *In the British Grand Prix of 1983
Prost drove a magnificent race, getting ahead
of the Ferraris by lap 15, and eventually
winning by a comfortable 20 seconds in the
RE40.*

Below: *At Silverstone Alain consolidated his lead in the World Championship, and here acknowledges the cheers, flanked by Piquet (left) and Tambay, second and third respectively.*

'After Zeltweg, where I won, I was 14 points ahead, with four races left. And afterwards the Renault people thought I was crazy when I said we would lose the championship to Brabham: the BMW engine suddenly had a *lot* more power from somewhere, and Renault didn't respond. Look, I said, we can't get pole position anywhere, because our engine won't accept a lot of boost, so Piquet will always be ahead of us on the grid – and with his horsepower he'll be impossible to pass in the race.

'That was why I took so much risk at Zandvoort, when I hit Nelson, trying to pass him. He was faster in the straights, but my car was better in the corners; over the lap, in fact, he was holding me up – and Arnoux's Ferrari was catching both of us. I had to take a chance, and it didn't work.'

Piquet won as he pleased at both Monza and Brands Hatch, which meant that the title would be settled at Kyalami. Arnoux was also in with a shout, but realistically the fight was between Renault and Brabham-BMW.

At Spa (above right) Prost and the Ferraris of Tambay and Arnoux could do nothing about de Cesaris's Alfa in the early stages, but when the Italian retired Alain won from Patrick. Right: In Austria the old rivals met again, Prost passing Arnoux's Ferrari for the win in the last five laps.

Dissatisfaction with Renault apart, Prost's life was in further turmoil. Italy – who saw him as the obstacle separating Arnoux from the World Championship – took against him with particular venom. Was René not a Ferrari driver? Was Alain not already his enemy? Before Monza there were anonymous letters, telephone calls, even kidnap threats. Over the Italian Grand Prix weekend, Renault hired bodyguards to protect their man, which did nothing to lessen the hatred of the *tifosi*. Prost, already hounded in France, immediately decided to move his family to Switzerland. At the same time, somewhat against his better judgement, he re-signed with Renault for 1984.

He felt no pressure, he said, in South Africa, because he went there in the knowledge that only luck would win him the World Championship. The Brabham-BMWs were on another level, he shrugged, and so they were. Never within striking distance of Piquet and Patrese, Prost retired from a distant third place with turbo failure.

Renault, in its infinite wisdom, had chosen to fly out to Johannesburg virtually every journalist capable of spelling the company's name. They were there to witness *le jour de la gloire*, and when it didn't happen there was nothing less than an inquisition afterwards. At the Elf motorhome Prost and Larrousse uncomfortably sat for an hour and more, being grilled by their disgruntled countrymen. Trouble was, it was awfully difficult to bite the hand...

Alain has never forgotten. 'You know what? Every week there is a house newspaper in the Renault factories, and after Kyalami it said I had stopped, not because there was a problem with the car, but because I was running only third and didn't want to look bad! There were also some French journalists who wrote the same sort of thing. Renault pushed too much. If they wanted to invite journalists to the race, OK; but journalists should always write what they truly think – which wasn't easy in the circumstances.'

Two days later, at a meeting back in Paris, Prost was fired by Renault, the Régie illogically choosing as scapegoat its greatest single asset. In three seasons Alain had won nine races in the yellow cars; they were never to win again.

'In fact, as it turned out, the Renault people did me a big favour. The situation had become impossible – I was very tired with the ridiculous amount of PR work I had to do for them. The guys who worked for the team were always good, but the organisation was so bad I despaired. There were too many bosses, and it was impossible to get anything done quickly, because there were too many people to

*The South African Grand Prix of '83 was
perhaps the most disagreeable of Prost's career.
In the RE40 he could do nothing to keep
Piquet's faster Brabham-BMW from stealing
the World Championship. It was to be his last
race in a Renault.*

Right: *First race after returning to McLaren – and victory. Prost describes the 1984 Brazilian Grand Prix as perhaps his most satisfying win.* Below right: *Elio de Angelis and Keke Rosberg, third and second respectively, join Alain on the rostrum.*

convince and persuade. And if you can't react quickly, you will never beat people like Ferrari and Brabham.

'It made me sad to realise how much hypocrisy there was in Formula 1. By the time I left Renault, I was on my guard the whole time, always wondering if that hand slapping me on the back had a dagger in it.'

If Prost felt relief more than anything else at the divorce from Renault, the stark reality was that it was now late October, and he didn't have a drive for 1984. A few weeks earlier he had spoken with Ron Dennis about going to McLaren, and now the talks were resumed – on a very different basis: 'I had nothing else, and Ron knew it. It embarrasses me now that I signed for so little, but at the time I didn't care. I was away from Renault, and that was all that mattered.'

So began one of the greatest partnerships racing has known: Prost and McLaren, or, as Ron Dennis would prefer, McLaren and Prost. Right away Alain began to sense good things in his future. This was a team which went *racing*, a team whose only priority was to win. John Barnard was the designer, TAG (Porsche) the engine supplier, Niki Lauda the team-mate.

In traditional McLaren style, Barnard's new car, the MP4/2, was late – indeed there was time only for a shakedown test at Ricard before the cars were flown out to Brazil for the first race. On the aeroplane to Rio Prost could barely conceal his optimism; he had shattered the short-track record at Ricard, and no car had ever felt so good first time out.

And he won the race, too. As he crossed the line, both arms were jubilantly in the air, a gesture we would not see from him again until Adelaide in 1986.

'That win was very special to me,' he says to this day. 'Psychologically, it was important, because it stopped all the shit between Renault and me and the French press. I won the race, but if Renault had won, and I hadn't finished, the press would have put pressure on me. They are like that, some of them. If I'm honest, too, I have to admit there was an element of revenge in that day for me.

'The really incredible thing, though, was that the French public changed its attitude to me after that race. Now I was with a foreign team, and suddenly they were for me. It was the same with Michel Platini – when he transferred to an Italian club, he became much more popular than when he was playing in France!

'It's strange, you know, but the French don't really like winners. They prefer the second, the man who loses gloriously. The all-time favourite hero on the Tour de France is Raymond Poulidor – who never won it; but they never liked Jacques

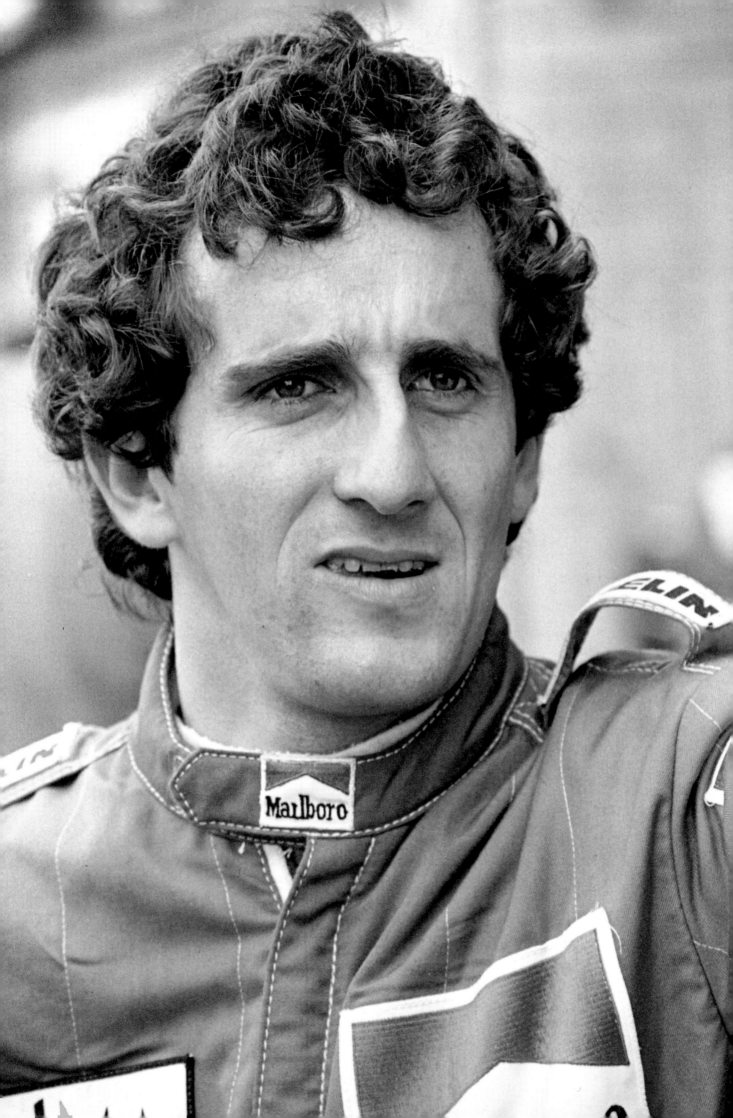

Anquetil, who won it five times!'

Prost loves his country, but without rose-tinted Gallic spectacles. 'It's a great day for France!' one of the journalists would say as Alain stepped from his car at Brands Hatch in 1985, the race which clinched his first World Championship. 'That irritated me. I said, "Look, I've won the championship in an English car, with a German engine, American tyres and sponsorship. Today I celebrate for *me*! Next week we can think about France."'

All that lay ahead, however. For now Alain had to acclimatise to life with Lauda, life with a McLaren team revamped and revitalised since he had left it in 1980. Teddy Mayer, to Prost's relief, was long gone. 'Now it's completely different – a good team, good car, good feeling. Perfect, in fact.'

The superiority of McLaren-TAG in 1984 surprised everyone in the business, not least the team itself. Prost's win in Brazil was only the first of *seven* he was to take that year, and it could quite easily have been ten. Lauda added five more to the tally.

Left: *After the frustrations of Renault, Prost
was relieved to move, finding new motivation
with McLaren, a team devoted above all to
winning Grands Prix. To his astonishment,
Alain found himself far more popular in
France once he had ceased driving for a French
team. At Monaco (above) he happily signed
autographs before going on to win the race.*

On raw speed, Niki was rarely a match for Alain, although in the races there was often little to choose. Where the younger man scored primarily was in qualifying, Lauda quite often starting three or four rows behind him. This gave the Austrian a lot to do, but very often he methodically worked through to second or, if anything happened to his team-mate, the lead.

'I just can't *believe* Alain in qualifying,' Niki said in Monte Carlo. Four years later Prost would be saying the same of Senna.

Lauda was wary of Prost at first, but soon came to appreciate him. 'All my suspicions disappeared,' Niki said, 'and I came to realise he was simply warm, friendly and straightforward. Not devious at all. My relationship with Ron Dennis, though, got worse and worse – the McLaren "ice age" I call it. Somehow he swung the whole team around behind Prost, but Alain was never part of that. Our relationship was always good.'

'The McLaren ice age'; Prost himself would come to understand the meaning of those words in 1989. What he would assuredly not have was the support and friendship of his team-mate as he endured it.

Alain's only controversial win of the year was at Monaco; controversial because appalling weather led to the stopping of the race, when Prost was leading, but being swiftly reeled in by Senna's Toleman – which was itself being caught by Stefan Bellof's Tyrrell.

Inevitably, there were suggestions that the clerk of the course (Jacky Ickx, a Porsche sports car driver) called a halt to proceedings so that Prost, using a Porsche engine, would win.

'I couldn't believe people would suggest something like that,' Alain says, 'but I tell you one thing: if racing drivers were intelligent – and if less money was involved in Formula 1 – for sure we would never have started that race. I was on the pole, and if I'd spun on the hill on the first lap – like Mansell did later – maybe 20 cars would have crashed. At first it was just slippery and unpleasant, but later, when the rain had really come down again, the visibility was ridiculous, a joke.'

Because the race was ended so prematurely, the points were halved, Prost scoring four and a half for his victory. That half would later come to haunt him.

Through the season he won more races than Lauda, yes, but Niki's finishing record was better. And the issue appeared settled at Monza, where the Austrian won, while Alain blew up. The gap, with two races left, was nine points. And a half.

*Monaco 1984. In the early stages Prost leads
from Mansell's Lotus. The Englishman later
took the lead, then crashed, and soon
afterwards the race was halted prematurely,
due to the terrible conditions. Alain won.*

Below: *Going into the Dutch Grand Prix*
Alain knew his only championship rival was
the man in the other McLaren.

Above right: *Hockenheim brought Prost his*
fourth win of 1984, with team-mate Lauda
just three seconds adrift. Right: *Despite*
losing the championship by half a point to
Niki, Alain was not too downhearted at
Estoril. In the evening of the race they
celebrated with Mansour Ojjeh of TAG.

Left: *Nürburgring 1984. Prost knew,
realistically, that to beat Lauda for the title he
had to win the last two races. The first of
them, the Grand Prix of Europe, he took
without problem.*

Below: *The faces tell the tale. In Portugal,
Prost has won the race, but Lauda the title.
And third man Senna ponders the future: the
next race at Estoril will be his.* Below left:
*Alain's drive in Portugal was magnificent. In
his quest for the title, he could have done
nothing more.*

At the Nürburgring, for the Grand Prix of Europe, Prost led all the way, with Lauda a poor fourth. Three points. And a half.

The situation at Estoril was therefore clear: Alain had simply to go for it, in the hope that Niki would finish lower than second. What he faced, in fact, was precisely the situation which confronted Stirling Moss in his battle with Mike Hawthorn at Casablanca in the last GP of the 1958 season.

Moreover the race turned out exactly the same way. Prost – and Moss – dominated; Lauda – and Hawthorn – finished a rather fortunate second. Between the McLarens, until 18 laps from the flag, was Mansell's Lotus. Had it not lost its brakes, Prost would have won the World Championship. But it did, and he didn't. By half a point.

On the rostrum, though, he somehow smiled. He had driven a magnificent race, could have done nothing more, and even Lauda sympathised. 'Don't worry,' he said, 'next year will be yours.'

Overleaf: *Zandvoort 1984. The fifth of
Prost's seven victories that year – but again
Lauda was second, banking six more points.*

Below: *Prost quickly developed an excellent
relationship with McLaren's chief designer,
John Barnard, who regards the Frenchman as
the greatest driver with whom he has worked.*

It was. Only five wins this time, but the major opposition – Senna (Lotus-Renault), Alboreto (Ferrari), Rosberg and Mansell (Williams-Honda) – did not have the reliability of the McLaren-TAG, so that Prost had the title locked away with two races to spare. To be sure of it, indeed, he uncharacteristically drove 'for points' at Spa and Brands Hatch. It went against the grain.

'To be honest, I did that because I wanted to get the World Championship settled and out of the way. In the two previous years I lost it at the last race, and I did *not* want that to happen again. Because I had been so close so many times, it had become too important to me, both in my career and my life.

Right: *Another triumph at Rio. Prost began
the '85 season as he had the one before.
Michele Alboreto (left) finished second for
Ferrari, and would be Alain's main rival for
the title through the year.*

Left: *Prost, here leading Rosberg's Williams-Honda, comfortably won the Austrian Grand Prix in 1985, leading all the way from pole position.* Below: *Not just now, please. Ron Dennis with his two drivers in 1985, the year of Lauda's retirement.*

'At Spa I was fastest in all four practice sessions, and the car was perhaps the best I've ever known. Almost perfect. And if the weather had been good, I would have won. Later in the race, when the line dried, I got fastest lap without problem.

'I wanted to go for the win, become champion in style, but it was the kind of day when anything could have happened – I nearly hit Piquet when he spun at the first corner, for example. Then they told me on the radio that Alboreto – my only rival for the title – was out, so then I decided to be prudent. I don't enjoy driving that way, but I don't regret it: Rosberg did exactly the same at Vegas in '82, and Piquet at Kyalami the year after.

'The point is, however much I hate to drive *tactique* races, I would have been World Champion before if I'd done that occasionally, like Niki did last year.'

Ironically, Alain's best fight of the year was with his team-mate. Generally, Lauda's car's reliability was appalling in 1985, and his motivation was considerably on the wane. But at Zandvoort neither faltered. Prost led convincingly at the half-way point, but a disastrously slow tyre stop dropped him to third, behind Lauda and Senna. After disposing of the Lotus, he clawed up to Niki.

The last ten laps or so were unforgettable. Team-mates they may have been, and friends, too, but their battle was ferocious. Perhaps Niki, having already announced his retirement, realised he would never be in this position again; whatever, he drove as nowhere else that year. Through the all-important Bos Uit, the right-hander onto the long pit straight, Prost's car was disturbed by the turbulence from Lauda's, with the consequence that Alain was never quite close enough to put a move on Niki into Tarzan. Two-tenths separated them at the finish.

Left: *Alain and Niki had a fantastic scrap in the late stages of the race at Zandvoort, the Austrian just holding on for his only win of the year – and the last of a great career.*

If Prost had lost the title by fewer than nine points, he would have looked back to Imola with even greater sorrow. 'I was proud of the job I did there, although it was not truly a race because fuel economy played such a big part. But I fought with Senna as long as I could – until I knew I had to back off, or run out. Maybe he could run the whole race at that speed, and finish – I didn't know. All I did know was that I couldn't.'

Neither could Senna, who duly ran dry before the end. It happened also to Prost, but not until his slowing-down lap. 'I calculated the fuel absolutely right, or so I thought. I think I drove that whole race as fast as it could have been done on 220 litres.'

Dry of fuel, the car failed its post-race weigh-in. With a small bag of potatoes added, it would have passed. After receiving the trophy, waving to the crowds, Alain took the news hard. An Italian photographer, trying to freeze the moment, spun him round, and for a second I thought Prost was going to clobber him.

There was no sign of 'the Professor' in that moment. This was an emotional racer who felt he had been robbed. Prost can be very direct. When, a year earlier, the British Grand Prix had been fatuously stopped after an unimportant accident, he stormed up to Jean-Marie Balestre to tell him in words of one syllable (and four letters) what he thought.

Still, the title was won, and suddenly Prost was to realise how popular he had become in his own land: the first French World Champion. 'The incredible thing', Patrick Tambay remarked, 'is that Alain is *still* underrated! Some people think he's lucked into everything.

'You know,' Tambay went on, 'there is all this talk about "natural talent" – a gift for driving race cars. And I suppose we must all have it in different degrees. But during my time in racing there have been three with something extra: Villeneuve, Senna, Prost. And maybe that "something extra" was different in each case. I don't know what this special quality is – only that it exists.'

Over that winter Prost did not get to relax as much as he would have wished. The PR machine was in full spate, and everywhere there were public appearances, interviews, whistle-stop tours. He found time to celebrate his championship with a trip to Bordeaux, where he visited several vineyards, buying cases of first growths. But when, in February, he arrived in Rio for testing he admitted he felt tired and jaded.

'As soon as I was back at a track, though, in my car, and working with the engineers again, all the fatigue disappeared. It was so good to be *driving* again, doing the work I enjoy, away from all the bullshit.'

Prost won his second Monaco Grand Prix in 1985, but had a difficult race, a sticking wastegate making his engine behave unpredictably.

'A bonus' was how Prost described his win at Monza (above), the McLaren outpaced by Rosberg's Williams-Honda, which retired in the late stages.

Right: By 1985 Alain's fascination with golf had taken hold. Far right: With Steve Nichols, one of McLaren's leading engineers. The two now work together at Ferrari.

Prost's two English races in 1985 brought differing successes. At Silverstone (right) he won the British Grand Prix after a long fight with Senna's Lotus, and at Brands Hatch (below right) he clinched his first World Championship, despite finishing only fourth in the Grand Prix of Europe.

Above: *That first title, after so many disappointments, meant a lot to Alain. 'More than anything,' he said, 'I feel relief that it's out of the way...'*

Kyalami 1985. Prost, here leading Lauda,
could do nothing about the Williams-Hondas
of Mansell and Rosberg, and finished only
third. The title, fortunately, was already won.

*Zandvoort 1981. Prost got the better of
Jones's Williams in a straight fight, scoring
his second Grand Prix win conclusively.*

In the Renault RE40 Prost should have won the 1983 World Championship. He won four races, more than any other driver, but in the end was beaten by the complacency of his own team.

Back to McLaren for 1984. At Zeltweg
(above) Prost was running second, but
spun off on de Angelis's oil while driving
one-handed – top gear was jumping out,
and he had to hold it in. Right: At
Zandvoort there were no problems. Alain
started from the pole, and won easily from
team-mate Lauda.

Pages 70-71: Brands Hatch 1985. In the
European Grand Prix Prost drove a
tactique race of the kind he hates. It went
against the grain to cruise for points, but the
title had previously eluded him too many
times. At Brands fourth place made him
World Champion.

In many ways 1986 was perhaps Alain's greatest season, for he kept his title, despite the presence of the faster Williams-Hondas. Left: At Monte Carlo he was simply majestic, taking pole position and leading all the way.

There was another victory in Austria (left), this time coping with an engine which repeatedly cut out. In Adelaide (above) Prost produced a mesmeric comeback drive after picking up a puncture, taking the lead in the closing stages – and retaining his World Championship.

By 1987 the TAG engine was outclassed by the Honda, and the season produced 'only' three wins for Prost. The last of them, at Estoril (left), was significant, however, since it was his 28th Grand Prix victory. At last Jackie Stewart's long-held record was beaten.

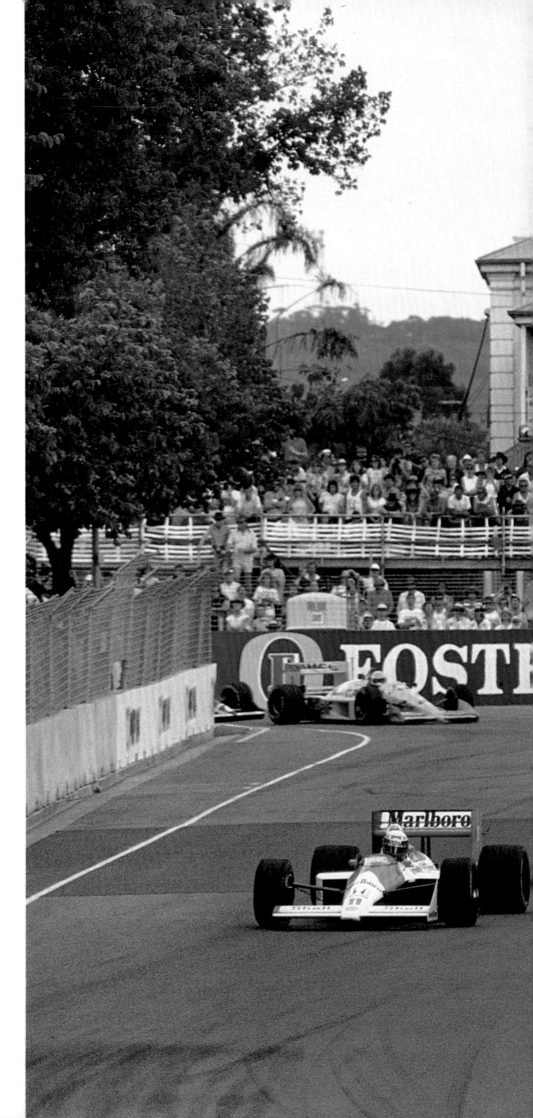

Prost lost the 1988 World Championship by the closest of margins to his new McLaren team-mate, Ayrton Senna, in Japan. Two weeks later, though, he finished the year with a clear-cut victory – his seventh of the season – in Adelaide. The Brazilian was second.

Alain did not enjoy his final season with McLaren, 1989. There was considerable dissension between Senna and himself, and he admits he rarely drove at his best. It was, nevertheless, enough to make him World Champion for the third time. At Spa (top) Prost fought hard with Mansell's Ferrari in the closing laps, holding on to second place. Above: *The controversial coming-together with Senna at Suzuka, which settled the title on the spot.*

Top: *Alain's wife Anne-Marie, here holding their son Nicolas, has little interest in motor racing, and has rarely seen her husband race.* Above: *In 1990 Prost is a Ferrari driver, and here tests a 640 at Estoril in preparation for the first race.* Right: *After all those years in McLaren overalls, the Prancing Horse badge takes a little getting used to. As the season approached, Prost declared his motivation well and truly back.*

*For 1986 Prost's McLaren team-mate was
Rosberg, and the two got along famously.
However, Keke was never able to adapt his
flamboyant style to suit the MP4/2.*

Lauda, now, was into permanent retirement, so for 1986 Prost had a new team-mate, one K. Rosberg. They had always got along, and their friendship strengthened as they worked together. However, where Niki's style had been very similar to Alain's, Keke's was entirely different. It had served him well at Williams, but his inability to modify it to suit the characteristics of the McLaren was a source of...constant irritation to John Barnard. Prost and Lauda had always raced with virtually identical settings; for Rosberg they didn't work.

A highlight of the previous season had been Keke's shattering 160 mph pole-position lap at Silverstone, and for many there had always been the suspicion that, while Prost might be the best in the business, Rosberg was the out-and-out quickest. The prospect was intriguing: how would Keke's blistering speed, always so overt, so apparent, stand up to the silky style of Alain?

The results tell the tale. In a season when the McLaren-TAGs were outpowered by the Williams-Hondas, Prost won four times, Rosberg not at all. And, in light of their supposed strengths, perhaps more significant is that Alain *out-qualified* Keke 12–4.

Left: *For much of the 1986 San Marino
Grand Prix the McLarens of Prost* (leading)
*and Rosberg fought a torrid battle with
Senna's Lotus.* Below left: *Alain finally
won at Imola, having judged his fuel
consumption perfectly. Berger's Benetton,
lapped but third, takes the flag behind him.
On the rostrum* (below) *Prost sprays the
Moët, flanked by second man Piquet* (left)
and Berger.

McLaren's MP4/2 was always inherently an understeering car, which admirably suited both Prost and Lauda, but steadfastly resisted the brake-as-late-as-possible-and-pitch-it-in style which had served Rosberg so well in Patrick Head's cars. As well as that, 1986 was the last year of unrestricted turbo boost, and Keke was never Alain's match in juggling revs, fuel and boost over a 200-mile race. It was a highly frustrating season for him, all in all.

For Prost, too, it was hard. Honda's power advantage was demonstrable, and in some races Mansell and Piquet were on their own, in a separate event. It was fortunate for the rest that they inevitably took points from each other – fortunate, too, that they gave little impression of driving for the same team.

Grey cells won Imola for Prost, who simply balanced his fuel consumption and pace better than anyone else. Rosberg ran dry towards the end.

Below: *Monaco '86 was perhaps the most convincing and dominant Grand Prix win of Alain's career. From pole position he ran away from team-mate Rosberg* (right) *and third man Senna.*

At Monte Carlo Alain had perhaps the most straightforward victory of his career. It was a day when he made the rest look clumsy and flat-footed. He started from pole position, and you noted he was using minimal revs, changing up early, keeping away from the kerbs. It was the others, bouncing from one apex to the next, who put his art into true perspective. Rosberg was a flamboyant second, Senna third.

Spa that year Prost believes he would have won without problem, had he not been delayed by a first-corner accident triggered by Senna, who came out of it unscathed. While Ayrton raced away to an eventual second place, Alain crawled, tyre flat, round Spa's long lap to the pits. After the car had been checked over, he rejoined in 23rd place, almost a lap back.

A touch of opposite lock next time through indicated we were in for something special, and by the finish he was up to sixth, having driven the fastest race of the afternoon.

John Barnard always cites this as the greatest drive he has ever seen: 'When he came in, we were satisfied the car was safe, but it certainly wasn't in A1 condition – we knew that when we found bent engine mountings afterwards. The thing was like a banana!'

Right: *Spa '86, the race which drew from Prost what John Barnard calls 'the greatest drive I've ever seen by anyone'. At the first corner* (inset) *the McLaren leaps over Berger's spinning Benetton, while Senna rushes away in the lead.* Main picture: *Alain came back from last to sixth, setting the fastest lap in a damaged car.*

Left: *When Prost ran out of fuel on the last
lap of the German Grand Prix, he gained
nothing by pushing the McLaren up to the
finish line – save highlighting the stupidity of
the limited fuel rule.*

Prost, it transpired, had needed an eighth of a turn of lock in a straight line…

'What's more,' John added, 'he never touched the boost, although the temptation must have been tremendous.'

After the race Alain pointed out that maybe that single point would be crucial by the end of the season. 'I lost the title in 1984 by half a point, you know, and something like that makes a big impression on you.'

He did not waste angry words on Senna, who had barged across the nose of Berger's Benetton at the first corner, pushing it into the McLaren. Instead, Ayrton was to learn a lesson in Montreal two weeks later.

In the early laps the Lotus was holding up a bunch led by Prost, and Alain got by with what had to be the passing manoeuvre of the season. Through the flat right-left-right swerves after the pits the McLaren drew alongside – then chopped across the Lotus to claim the line. It was fair, yet as ruthless as anything you will see.

Virtually everywhere that season we saw something outstanding from the reigning World Champion. His competitiveness was as fierce as ever, which greatly impressed Jackie Stewart.

'Undoubtedly there's an infectious disease which afflicts every World Champion and his team, and it's been going on for years. It's not right to say that the guy who's champion loses his edge, or that the designer relaxes, the mechanics lose interest or whatever. But somewhere along the line these things occur – I'm talking about decimal points, but they all add up. The record book shows that hardly ever have a driver and team won back-to-back titles: Fangio did it with Mercedes, and Brabham with Cooper, and that's it.

'So it's *that* aspect of Prost and McLaren that so impresses me,' Stewart said. 'As for Alain himself…well, I used to think he and Piquet were on a par, but not any more. Nelson's car is undoubtedly quicker, but he's making a lot of mistakes. Prost, on the other hand, makes incredibly few errors. For me, he's the best driver in the world, no argument.'

Alain never relaxed during 1986. At the Österreichring he won with a car whose engine repeatedly cut out as soon as the power was off. Several times he approached the Hella-Licht chicane in silence, then found a lower gear, dropped the clutch and revived the engine. The same problem eliminated Rosberg. At Monza there was a mesmeric drive from pit lane to sixth in 19 laps – and then the black flag for switching too late to the T-car.

Despite the strength of his performances, however, Prost was not his usual smiling

In Austria (left) *there was another win for
Alain, despite persistent engine problems.*

self for much of the season. In Austria, indeed, he said he was seriously considering a sabbatical in 1987, then returning the following year.

'A lot of things were wrong at the time,' he says. 'For one thing, the atmosphere in the team wasn't very pleasant, because Dennis and Barnard weren't getting on, and there were arguments all the time. We were having a very hard time against the Hondas, and I began to think, "If you are not absolutely competitive, maybe stopping for a year would be the right thing to do – then you can concentrate on your private problems, try to fix them, then come back." I didn't *want* to stop, but I thought maybe it would be the best compromise for me. I was lucky that everything turned out well – with the car, anyway...'

Although Alain rarely spoke of it, his life that summer was overwhelmed by thoughts of his brother, Daniel, who had cancer and was dying. He succumbed to the illness the day before qualifying began in Estoril.

In the race Prost hung back from the battle between Piquet and Senna, focusing on his fuel read-out. After Nelson had obligingly spun, and Ayrton run dry on the last lap, along came Alain for six more points. Only through this kind of discipline was he able to go into the last two races with a chance of the title.

That weekend he was understandably at the track as little as possible; Daniel's funeral came two days later.

By now Barnard had left McLaren. 'I was disappointed he did it then,' Alain says, 'because there were four races to go, and we still had a chance in the championship.'

In Mexico he was on five cylinders for much of the race, dared not come in for fear of stalling, and so got through the race on only two sets of tyres. On the rough surface Piquet's otherwise healthy Williams needed four. Alain took six points from the day, Nelson three.

More significantly, Mansell was left at the start, and scored only two points on a day when he might have clinched the title. Still, the odds were firmly with him in Adelaide. He had 70 points to Prost's 64 and Piquet's 63, and to become World Champion needed only to finish third – whatever happened to his rivals. For Alain and Nelson, therefore, only one policy would do: go for it.

So often to travel is better than to arrive, but the 1986 Australian Grand Prix stands as perhaps the most stirring race of the decade. In unexpectedly cold conditions Mansell took the pole, with Piquet next to him, then Senna. Prost was fourth, Rosberg seventh, the Finn promising to do everything possible to help his teammate.

Prost could do nothing about Mansell's
Williams-Honda in the Portuguese Grand
Prix, but finished second, ahead of Piquet's
similar car.

'I've never known why,' Keke says, 'but on race morning my car was simply transformed – it was something I could *drive* at last. We hadn't touched it, but suddenly it turned in like a dream, which had never happened before. I began to believe my last race could be good.'

It was more than that. In the course of an awesome first lap, there were no fewer than three leaders, first Mansell, then Senna, then Piquet. Rosberg was fourth at the end of it, second a lap later, into the lead on lap seven! And thereafter he went away from the pack, leaving everyone convinced he could not make the finish at that rate.

Prost, aided by an understandably cautious Mansell and a spinning Piquet, moved up to second place and, mindful of his team-mate's promise, was looking good for a win. But on lap 32 he clipped Berger's Benetton, and punctured a front tyre, rejoining in fourth place, title hopes apparently dead.

Alain did not see it that way, however. In the morning Goodyear had recommended a routine tyre change to all its teams, and Prost accepted the advice.

The great day in Adelaide. Left: *Both arms are in the air as Alain takes an unexpected win in the Australian Grand Prix, thereby stealing the World Championship from the Williams drivers.* Below left: *Piquet smiles graciously in defeat as Prost celebrates his triumph. Johansson* (right) *was third for Ferrari.*

'I talked to the Goodyear guys for a long time, and I was fairly sure a non-stop run would mean problems with wear. So I agreed with the team I would stop on lap 43.

'To be honest, I almost changed my mind before the race: after all, if the others were not stopping, maybe I should do the same…but from work in practice I knew I was quite marginal – and my car was always better on tyres than the Williams.'

On his fresh tyres Prost began to charge, while in the pits Williams personnel consulted the Goodyear engineers, who had examined Alain's original set. On the strength of that, Mansell and Piquet were advised to keep going, albeit with some circumspection.

On lap 63, with 19 to go, there was no Rosberg: his right-rear tyre had come apart. Piquet was now elevated to the lead, with Prost up to second, and Mansell where he needed to be, third. But Keke's tyre failure threw Williams into a quandary: should they bring Nelson and Nigel in?

They did not have time to act. A lap later Mansell's left-rear exploded on the flat-out Dequetteville Terrace, which left a straight fight between Piquet and Prost: suddenly winning the race meant winning the World Championship. And Alain was reeling Nelson in.

In light of what had befallen Mansell, Frank Williams and Patrick Head had to bring Piquet in, with 17 laps left. Hence Prost took the lead. In the closing laps the Williams, now on new tyres, began to catch the McLaren: Alain was worried about fuel.

'My read-out had been five litres "the wrong side" since half-way through the race, but that day there was no point in cutting revs and boost – I *had* to win, or it was finished. All I could do was hope the read-out was wrong.' Clearly, it was, for he made it to the flag, Piquet only four seconds behind.

As he crossed the line, both arms were in the air, and when he climbed from the McLaren you could sense the joy he felt. After saluting the crowd he threw his gloves into the cockpit, in a gesture which said, 'Well, how about that?' As he fumbled with the strap of his helmet, you could see – even through the letter-box opening – the joy on his face, and as he walked across the road to the pits he was shaking his head in disbelief.

Later, much later, Rosberg would tip Prost for another World Championship in 1987. 'There can't be as many engine problems as we've had this year,' Keke reasoned. 'I mean, he had *no* chance this year – and he still won it!

Left: *Start as you mean to go on. Alain began
1987 in his traditional fashion, with victory
in Brazil. New team-mate Johansson was
third, behind Piquet's Williams.*

'Alain', he said, 'is the best driver I've ever seen. As an all-round driver, he's head and shoulders clear of anyone else because he's strong in every department. There's Prost, and then the rest. And I like him as a bloke as much as I rate him as a driver.'

The following year, now retired, Rosberg came to most races as a TV commentator. He found the role of spectator fascinating, and also revealing.

'That McLaren understeers like a pig!' he exclaimed. 'Only Prost can drive it properly. I've been watching him closely, and his technique is totally different from anyone else's.

'I always drove the "standard" way: brake as late as possible, get into the corner, back on the power as soon as possible. Alain's not like that at all. He's very early on the brakes – but only lightly. And while he's braking, he's turning in, right up to the apex sometimes. It's very smooth, very easy on the car and tyres, and *very* quick the way he does it. Last year I tried to copy him sometimes, during testing and so on, and it never worked for me. I was always slower than before.'

Unique style or not, Prost had a relatively thin time of it in 1987. With Stefan Johansson as his team-mate, he had a lot of fun, but there were only three victories in a year when you needed a Honda to be regularly competitive. Mansell and Piquet had the season virtually to themselves, but Alain scored a memorable victory at Estoril, forcing Berger's faster Ferrari into a spin towards the end. This, his 28th Grand Prix victory, finally took him past Stewart's long-time record.

Not only was the TAG no match for the Honda on power, it was also, by 1987, notably inferior on reliability. Alain was irritated that broken alternator belts put him out at Imola and Hockenheim, two races he believed he would have won, and elsewhere there were sundry electrical problems.

The best of Prost we saw at Suzuka, where he did not win – indeed, did not score. At the end of the first lap he was on the tail of Berger's Ferrari; next time around he was well last, crawling to the pits, punctured.

His comeback drive that day beggared description, the sort of thing in which Villeneuve would have gloried: going fast for the sake of it, showing what was possible when you were the best, and angry. Berger was an easy winner, under threat from no one, yet in the course of the race Prost made up almost a whole lap on him, his fastest lap almost two seconds better than anyone else. All for seventh place.

'I don't know why he became known as "the Professor",' commented Ron Dennis. 'Yes, he's a great test driver, but once you get him in a Grand Prix he's a hard, instinctive racer.'

*At Estoril (left) Prost drove brilliantly to
pressure Berger's Ferrari into a late spin,
Alain going on to score his record-breaking
28th Grand Prix win.*

Yes, certainly, but also by now a much more *dégagé* personality. Winning the World Championship the first time served to relax Alain a lot, and the second title continued the process. He still bit his nails, but now the haunted face of the Renault days was never seen. Rather than hang around at the track for hours at the end of each day, he now preferred to go off for a few holes of golf, which had become a passion. And, as he lightened up, so his driving became better yet.

'Early in my career I was completely obsessed – I could think about nothing but racing. It must have been very boring for my family and friends.' His wife, Anne-Marie, has never had any real interest in motor racing, but Nicolas, born in 1981, is increasingly fascinated by his father's job.

Prost loves most sports, and natural stamina has always been one of his great strengths. With the top of his driving suit peeled down, he looks more like a scrum-half than a racing driver. His forearms are like hams.

'I jog nearly every day when I'm home in Switzerland,' he says. 'Golf I love, of course, and I play as often as I can. Then there is tennis, some gymnastics…but I *never* do anything like that because I feel I must.'

What about boxing? someone said. Did that account for his crooked nose? 'Ah, *non*! It has been broken four times, you know. First time in a car accident on the road, second time showing the police how the accident happened…no, no, second time on roller skates, third time falling down stairs, fourth time falling off someone's shoulders…

'The secret of any sport is to enjoy it, and for me motor racing is still a sport. A few years ago I was a great fan of the English footballer, Kevin Keegan, not because he was the greatest player or anything, but because I liked watching a man so obviously enjoying what he was doing. That's the most important thing. When I stop enjoying racing, I will stop doing it.'

These sentiments were expressed in 1987; little did Alain then realise how much his life was going to change. At Monza it was announced that Honda engines would power the McLarens in 1988 and beyond; and coming with them was Ayrton Senna.

Prost had no real anxieties about the arrival of the Brazilian, beyond the suspicion that the fun quotient of his professional life – always abundant with Lauda, Rosberg and Johansson – was about to take a dive. After striving against Honda for three years, he had to be realistic.

The new team-mates' working relationship began shakily, at the Rio tests in

In 1988 Ayrton Senna arrived at McLaren. Initially Alain got on tolerably well with his new team-mate, but that situation was not to last.

early 1988. Alain considered 'the *arriviste*' was moving in a touch autocratically. Seeking to bridge the gap between Ayrton and humility, therefore, he decided to play a game.

They were sharing a car, the two of them, and the plan one day was for Prost to run through the afternoon, then hand over to Senna, who would 'go for a time' on new tyres. In came Alain, and on went the fresh Goodyears. Ayrton stood by, helmet on, but Alain stayed put. Only after noting Senna's agitation, hearing 'It's not fair…' did Prost pop the belts and alight, shaking with laughter. Senna missed the joke. Prost would come to take that for granted.

Still, they worked together well enough that first season, and in difficult circumstances, too, for it was swiftly apparent that the World Championship was off-limits to anyone not driving a McLaren-Honda. Steve Nichols's new car, the MP4/4, was a gem, and on horsepower no other engine was close. They had only each other to beat.

Right: *Detroit 1988. At the circuit he most
loathed, Prost could not keep pace with
Senna, and settled for an easy second.*

Probably, there will never again be a season so absolutely dominated by one team. In 16 races, McLaren-Honda contrived to lose only once. By July Ron Dennis offered the suggestion that probably the title would go to the man who won most races: it was as close as that. And he proved to be right. Prost's *finishing* record was better: seven wins, seven second places added up to 11 more points than eight wins, three seconds and a fourth. But under the 'best 11 scores' rule the title went to Senna.

Curiously enough, in light of the closeness of their fight, there was comparatively little actual *racing* between Alain and Ayrton. Such was the parity of their equipment that usually the man who won the race was the man who made the better start. In Mexico, France, Portugal, Spain and Australia Prost was untouchable; Montreal, Detroit, Silverstone, Hockenheim and Spa were all Senna. And in the vital deciding race, at Suzuka, Ayrton drove with surpassing brilliance to catch and beat Alain on a treacherously slippery track.

Prost accepted the situation with great equanimity. On the evening of the lost championship, in Japan, his humour was good, his smile intact. The worst aspect of it, he said, was the disappointment his son would be feeling back home in Switzerland.

As early as Spa, in August, he had apparently acknowledged that the championship was lost. The race had given Senna his fourth consecutive win, and at the post-race press conference Alain paid tribute to his team-mate: 'He has been the best driver this year; he deserves to be World Champion.' That rather took everyone's breath away.

In Portugal and Spain, however, Senna had no answer to Prost, and thus the championship came alive again. After the race in Estoril, though, Alain had sharp words for Ayrton's tactics. At the end of the first lap, as he slipstreamed past the Brazilian into the lead, Senna quite deliberately swerved at him, forcing him perilously close to the pit wall. 'If he wants the title as badly as that,' Prost said, 'he can have it.'

Later, in private, he made his feelings clear to Senna, after which the two men shook hands. 'I'm sure', said Alain at the end of the season, 'that winning the championship will have a good effect on Ayrton, as it did on me. He'll lighten up a bit, and enjoy his racing more.' This was one Prost forecast which would prove completely awry.

In Adelaide, for the first time, Alain had a row of some consequence with Ron

*The McLarens lead the pack into the first
corner of the Portuguese Grand Prix (right).
A lap later Senna would swerve at Prost, as
the Frenchman took the lead...*

Below: *Happier days. Prost and Ron Dennis*
were firm friends until the second half of 1989,
when Alain decided he was quitting McLaren
for Ferrari.

Dennis. He had anticipated that the McLaren boss would do everything possible to make Senna feel welcome in a new environment, and considered that reasonable enough; but hadn't it gone a little too far?

'At Monaco I was angry with Ron. Ayrton crashed, and I won the race. At the gala I made a small speech, and thought I was very nice about Ayrton, but there was only so far I could go, you know? Then Ron came on the podium....He was stupid, but sometimes that's him. He wanted to help Senna – too much. He said I was behind, and Ayrton was fantastic, and for sure he had a problem with the car because he couldn't have crashed because of a mistake, and things like that.

'It wasn't necessary to do that. What I had said was enough: that Senna had pole position, that it was his race, but it was part of the game, and I was very happy to win. But, no, Ron had to go further than that. Afterwards he admitted he'd been wrong, but...'

This Prost found irritating, but more so by far was Dennis's press conference in Australia, at which Alain's mechanical problems over the season were effectively glossed over. Afterwards he took Dennis to task, and Ron admitted that, yes, perhaps the team had bent over backwards to keep Ayrton happy and secure. And perhaps Prost never felt quite the same about McLaren from that day on.

Left: At Montreal in 1988 Prost led Senna
for 18 laps before the Brazilian passed him
under braking for the hairpin.

Left: *It was at Imola in 1989 that the Prost–*
Senna relationship began to disintegrate,
Ayrton passing Alain at the first corner, in
spite of his own suggestion that they should
not fight over it.

Still, the air had been cleared, Alain believed. There was the new season to think about, the beginning of the new normally aspirated Formula 1, the V10 engine from Honda, a new car designed by Neil Oatley.

This, the MP4/5, proved less 'driver-friendly' than its predecessor, being harder to set up, harder to drive. However, Honda's considerable power advantage was more than capable of offsetting any handling deficiencies, and no one doubted that McLaren would again do most of the winning.

Not in Rio, though. At the first corner Senna tangled with Berger's Ferrari, and Prost lost his clutch after the first of two planned tyre stops – which made stopping a second time out of the question. Therefore he had to nurse his tyres for twice the distance expected, as well as make clutchless changes for the rest of the afternoon. In the circumstances, second to Mansell's Ferrari was a great achievement, and Alain considered it one of the best drives of his life.

At Imola, though, Senna won, and this was the day when the relationship between the two McLaren drivers began to disintegrate. There was in Prost's driving that afternoon a visible anger that no one could recall before, and after the race he declined to make any comment to the press, beyond muttering about 'an agreement not being respected'.

Over the next few days the story broke: Senna had suggested to Prost they should not fight over the first corner on the opening lap: the man who led in should lead out. After that, when clear of the rest, they could get down to racing. Prost agreed and led down to the turn – where Senna overtook him. Alain was livid, probably as much as anything with himself, for being duped.

'I felt stupid, it's true, just as with Arnoux all those years ago at Ricard. When something like this happens, I just feel I want to get away from the whole business. The day after the race I called Ron Dennis, and told him I was thinking of stopping for the rest of the year.

'I remembered too much, you see, of what happened with Villeneuve and Pironi in '82. I was a friend of Didier, and even more of Gilles, and I spoke to Gilles a lot the week before he died, once or twice a day sometimes. Every time he talked about Didier, and he was *so* angry, I couldn't believe it. Then there was the accident, and I knew for sure what had happened. I told Ron I wasn't going to react to Senna, but I felt so bad, so demotivated, I might stop until the end of the year.'

He decided to go on, however, and at Monte Carlo said he would continue to work with Senna on a technical basis, but that otherwise he wanted nothing more

Prost's victory at Monza (left) *was received*
with rapture by the fans. That weekend his
signing for Ferrari had been announced.

to do with him. Ayrton walked away with the race, Alain taking second.

Mexico, two weeks later, was another comfortable Senna victory, with Prost an unhappy fourth, after choosing the wrong tyre compound at the start, then needing two stops. Everything looked to be going the Brazilian's way, and Prost seemed like a man demoralised, beaten.

The question of his future was frequently raised, not least by Ron Dennis, who was keen for Alain to renew his contract, due to expire at the end of the season. Senna's, on the other hand, had another year to run. Surely the prospect of continuing as his team-mate was untenable to Alain?

For endless weeks Prost dithered. A McLaren 'B' team was considered, even a year of Indy car racing, perhaps that sabbatical of which he had often talked. There were huge offers to go sports car racing from Mercedes and Peugeot. Finally, at Paul Ricard, Alain announced he would not drive for McLaren in 1990; beyond that, his plans were undecided.

Dennis and Mansour Ojjeh of TAG were both present at the press conference, and Ron stressed his belief that this was not the end of the McLaren–Prost story. Whatever, he said, their friendship would endure. The atmosphere was entirely amicable, if a touch sorrowful.

Inevitably, Alain was resentful at feeling obliged to leave what he had come to regard as 'his' team. 'Maybe', he said 'Ayrton and I should have settled this thing a different way.' And he related one of his best stories, of his karting days, of one François Goldstein.

'*Alors*, Goldstein. He was a very good driver, but not always very clean, you know? One day we were racing at a track near Paris, in a very important race, a round of the European Championship. I was leading by a long way, with Goldstein second, and on the last lap a friend of his – another Belgian – pushed me off the track as I lapped him. When I came back on it, Goldstein was right behind me, and at the last corner *he* pushed me off! And he won, with me second.

'After I crossed the line he held out his hand – he wanted to shake hands with me! We had had problems before, and I was furious. What you need to know is that the guy who won that race was also going to win a works drive with one of the Italian teams. Goldstein was rich, but I had nothing, so it was really important to me. I couldn't accept losing a race like that, so I got my kart behind his, and I pushed him, flat out in the straight – I was right on the limiter!

'Then we stopped, and I hit him. Not so easy, you know, because he was almost two metres tall. But I punched him in the face – I had to jump up to reach him! Maybe I did the wrong thing, but he wasn't correct, either. He pushed me off deliberately.

'We are good friends now,' Alain concluded, 'and I wonder if maybe that would have been the best solution with Ayrton. I'm quite serious. That might have been the best way of resolving it, because then perhaps we could have been friends afterwards, having settled it like men, you know?'

Instead, the McLaren season rumbled on with an increasing lack of harmony. The management could stand the thought that Alain Prost was leaving, but when the suggestion arose that he might go to Ferrari, they appeared to take the news ill. And, worse, they got extremely agitated when he began to suggest – as had other Honda drivers before him – that some engines (Senna's) appeared to be rather more equal than others (his own).

Whether or not Prost was right, he certainly *believed* he was right, and on occasion – notably at Mexico City and Monza – there indeed seemed a sound basis for his dissatisfaction. McLaren maintained that the two drivers were always given equal equipment, while Honda put Senna's greater speed down to his greater expertise with a normally aspirated engine.

Particularly frustrating for the team was that, through all this, Prost looked like winning his third World Championship. True enough, he was depressed and well short of his best, rarely matching Senna for pace, but he had better engine reliability than Ayrton (perhaps the legacy of using fewer revs?), and made no mistakes to speak of. Senna retired at Phoenix, Ricard and Silverstone; Prost won the lot.

By Monza the team was in a state of ferment. It was now known that Alain would be a Ferrari driver in 1990, causing the atmosphere in the McLaren motorhome to drop another ten degrees. And in the race Senna retired from the lead, leaving victory to Prost. On the rostrum he handed down one of the trophies to the *tifosi*, for whom he was now suddenly a hero. And Dennis, overcome with rage, dropped the other one at his driver's feet. Any remnant of friendship between the two was now gone.

For all concerned, the last four races together were something to be endured, nothing more. In Portugal and Spain Prost, in his own words, drove 'like a taxi driver', merely looking for points. And the situation, as they went to Suzuka, was that only a win would keep Senna in with a chance of retaining his title.

'I'm going to drive an aggressive race today,' Alain said in Japan. 'I want to win

*Prost drove at his very best to lead the 1989
Japanese Grand Prix (left). The controversy
that surrounded his subsequent clash with
Senna tended to overshadow Alain's
achievement in winning his third title.*

the championship by winning the race.' And he added, for Ayrton's benefit, that his days of leaving the door open were gone.

For the race Prost opted for a low-downforce set-up, reasoning that straightline speed was of paramount importance here, but Senna – on pole position, as usual – opted to run more wing.

Alain, notably relaxed on the grid, made one of the great starts of his life, and was into the lead before the first turn, after which he drove a quite stupefying opening lap. The early part of the race, indeed, was vintage Prost; after a dozen laps he was more than five seconds up on Senna, and out of the Brazilian's sight. Alain had not driven like this for a long time. Even when he hit traffic, where Ayrton was usually demonstrably quicker, the gap barely reduced.

Over the long haul, though, Senna gradually whittled down Prost's lead. Alain later claimed that he had Ayrton handled, and could have held him off, but the question was academic. With six laps to go, Senna tried to go by into the chicane, a ploy which can work only with the co-operation of the man being overtaken. And that, Prost had earlier made clear, was a thing of the past. The two cars touched, and the rest of the story is too well documented to bear repetition.

It was effectively the last time Alain would race a McLaren. Two weeks later, in Adelaide, he considered the torrential conditions unacceptable, and withdrew after a single lap. The lack of visibility, he said, was a joke, and he declined to race blind. Later, both Senna and Piquet would run into slower cars on the straight, simply because they were unable to see them.

How did Prost feel that afternoon? 'As if part of my life has come to an end,' he said. 'Yes, I'm looking forward to working for Ferrari at last – I think everyone dreams of driving for Ferrari at some time in their career. But I'm sorry my life at McLaren has finished this way. I suppose I always thought I would only leave here to retire. Sad, *hein*?

'I tell you one thing: I've learned a big lesson this year. It's the first time I've ever been in a weak position in a team, and I've seen things I never realised before – I never knew what John Watson was going through in 1980, for example, or how bad it must have been for Niki in '85, even for Keke the year after. I never realised how a team can control everything.

'Still,' he added, 'it's happened, and that's it. We have to look to the future, all of us. I can't wait to climb into a Ferrari for the first time.' Would his motivation come back? 'Yes,' he grinned. 'Oh, yes...'

Left: *Last McLaren day. In Adelaide Alain –
already confirmed as World Champion – looks
at the weather, and finds it unacceptable for
racing.*

ALAIN PROST · CAREER RECORD
BY JOHN TAYLOR

1976

	Race	Circuit	Date	Entrant	Car	Comment
1	Formula Renault France Championship	Le Mans	04/04/76	Renault-Elf Prost	Martini MK17-Renault	
1	Formula Renault France Championship	Nogaro	18/04/76	Renault-Elf Prost	Martini MK17-Renault	*Pole/Fastest lap*
1	Formula Renault France Championship	Magny Cours	01/05/76	Renault-Elf Prost	Martini MK17-Renault	*Pole/Fastest lap*
1	Formula Renault Europe – Heat 1	Dijon	09/05/76	Danielson Racing Team	Lola T410-Renault	
ret	Formula Renault Europe – Final	Dijon	09/05/76	Danielson Racing Team	Lola T410-Renault	*fuel leak/Pole*
ret	Formula Renault Europe	Zolder	16/05/76	Danielson Racing Team	Lola T410-Renault	*spun off*
1	Formula Renault France Championship	Clermont Ferrand	23/05/76	Renault-Elf Prost	Martini MK17-Renault	*Pole/Fastest lap*
1	Formula Renault France Championship	Folembray	20/06/76	Renault-Elf Prost	Martini MK17-Renault	*Pole*
1	Formula Renault France Championship	Rouen	27/06/76	Renault-Elf Prost	Martini MK17-Renault	*Fastest lap*
1	Formula Renault France Championship	Paul Ricard	04/07/76	Renault-Elf Prost	Martini MK17-Renault	*Fastest lap*
1	Formula Renault France Championship	Magny Cours	11/07/76	Renault-Elf Prost	Martini MK17-Renault	*Pole/Fastest lap*
1	Formula Renault France Championship	Dijon	05/08/76	Renault-Elf Prost	Martini MK17-Renault	*Pole/Fastest lap*
1	Formula Renault France Championship	Nogaro	19/08/76	Renault-Elf Prost	Martini MK17-Renault	*Fastest lap*
1	Formula Renault France Championship	Albi	30/09/76	Renault-Elf Prost	Martini MK17-Renault	*Fastest lap*
1	Formula Renault France Championship	Paul Ricard	17/10/76	Renault-Elf Prost	Martini MK17-Renault	*Fastest lap*
ret	Formula Renault France Championship	Imola	24/10/76	Renault-Elf Prost	Martini MK17-Renault	*fuel feed/Fastest lap*

1977

	Race	Circuit	Date	Entrant	Car	Comment
3	Formula Renault Europe Championship	Le Mans	27/03/77	Elf Racing	Martini MK20-Renault	
1	Formula Renault Europe Championship	Nogaro	11/04/77	Elf Racing	Martini MK20-Renault	*Fastest lap*
5	Formula Renault Europe Championship	Hockenheim	17/04/77	Elf Racing	Martini MK20-Renault	
1	Formula Renault Europe Championship	Magny Cours	01/05/77	Elf Racing	Martini MK20-Renault	
2	Formula Renault Europe Championship	Monte Carlo	22/05/77	Elf Racing	Martini MK20-Renault	*Fastest lap*
2	Formula Renault Europe Championship	Pau	29/05/77	Elf Racing	Martini MK20-Renault	*Fastest lap*
ret	Formula Renault Europe Championship	Zolder	05/06/77	Elf Racing	Martini MK20-Renault	*engine/Pole*
3	Formula Renault Europe Championship	Clermont Ferrand	19/06/77	Elf Racing	Martini MK20-Renault	
1	Formula Renault Europe Championship	Rouen	26/06/77	Elf Racing	Martini MK20-Renault	*Pole/Fastest lap*
13	Formula Renault Europe Championship	Dijon	03/07/77	Elf Racing	Martini MK20-Renault	
10	Grand Prix de Nogaro (F2)	Nogaro	10/07/77	Willi Kauhsen Racing Team	Elf 2J-Renault	
1	Formula Renault Europe Championship	Nogaro	10/07/77	Elf Racing	Martini MK20-Renault	*Pole*
ret	Formula Renault Europe Championship	Magny Cours	17/07/77	Elf Racing	Martini MK20-Renault	*gearbox/Pole*
5	Formula Renault Europe Championship	Paul Ricard	24/07/77	Elf Racing	Martini MK20-Renault	
1	Formula Renault Europe Championship	Monza	11/09/77	Elf Racing	Martini MK20-Renault	*Fastest lap*
1	Formula Renault Europe Championship	Albi	25/09/77	Elf Racing	Martini MK20-Renault	*Fastest lap*
ret	Grande Premio do Estoril (F2)	Estoril	02/10/77	Willi Kauhsen Racing Team	Elf 2J-Renault	*lost wheel*
7	Formula Renault Europe Championship	Paul Ricard	15/10/77	Elf Racing	Martini MK20-Renault	*Fastest lap*

1978

	Race	Circuit	Date	Entrant	Car	Comment
10	European Formula 3 Championship	Zolder	23/04/78	ORECA	Martini MK21B-Renault	
4	Grand Prix de Monaco Formula 3	Monte Carlo	07/05/78	ORECA	Martini MK21B-Renault	
ret	Pau Grand Prix (F2)	Pau	15/05/78	Fred Opert Racing	Chevron B40-Hart	*engine*
ret	European Formula 3 Championship	Nürburgring	28/05/78	ORECA	Martini MK21B-Renault	*engine*
10	European Formula 3 Championship	Dijon	04/06/78	ORECA	Martini MK21B-Renault	
14	European Formula 3 Championship	Monza	25/06/78	ORECA	Martini MK21B-Renault	
3	BP Formula 3 Championship	Paul Ricard	02/07/78	ORECA	Martini MK21B-Renault	
ret	European Formula 3 Championship	Magny Cours	16/07/78	ORECA	Martini MK21B-Renault	*engine*
6	European Formula 3 Championship	Donington Park	26/08/78	ORECA	Martini MK21B-Renault	
3	Vandervell Formula 3 Championship	Silverstone	28/08/78	ORECA	Martini MK21B-Renault	
1	European Formula 3 Championship	Járama	17/09/78	ORECA	Martini MK21B-Renault	*Pole/Fastest lap*
ret	European Formula 3 Championship	Vallelunga	08/10/78	ORECA	Martini MK21B-Renault	*engine*

1979

	Race	Circuit	Date	Entrant	Car	Comment
2	European Formula 3 Championship	Vallelunga	18/03/79	ORECA	Martini MK27-Renault	*Fastest lap*
1	European Formula 3 Championship	Österreichring	16/04/79	ORECA	Martini MK27-Renault	
1	European Formula 3 Championship	Zolder	23/04/79	ORECA	Martini MK27-Renault	
1	European Formula 3 Championship	Magny Cours	01/05/79	ORECA	Martini MK27-Renault	*Fastest lap*
3	European Formula 3 Championship	Donington Park	20/05/79	ORECA	Martini MK27-Renault	
1	Grand Prix de Monaco Formula 3	Monte Carlo	26/05/79	ORECA	Martini MK27-Renault	*Pole/Fastest lap*
1	European Formula 3 Championship	Zandvoort	04/06/79	ORECA	Martini MK27-Renault	*Pole/Fastest lap*
ret	European Formula 3 Championship	Monza	24/06/79	ORECA	Martini MK27-Renault	*driveshaft*
14	Vandervell Formula 3 Championship	Silverstone	14/07/79	ORECA	Martini MK27-Renault	*1-min. pen./pit stop/tyre*
1	European Formula 3 Championship	Knutstorp	05/08/79	ORECA	Martini MK27-Renault	*Pole/Fastest lap*
ret	European Formula 3 Championship	Kinnekulle	12/08/79	ORECA	Martini MK27-Renault	*engine/Pole*
1	European Formula 3 Championship	Járama	09/09/79	ORECA	Martini MK27-Renault	*Pole/Fastest lap*
1	Formula 3 Race	La Châtre	15/09/79	ORECA	Martini MK27-Renault	*Fastest lap*
1	Formula 3 Race	Albi	22/09/79	ORECA	Martini MK27-Renault	*Fastest lap*

1980

6	ARGENTINE GP	Buenos Aires	13/01/80	Marlboro Team McLaren	McLaren M29B-Cosworth DFV	
5	BRAZILIAN GP	Interlagos	27/01/80	Marlboro Team McLaren	McLaren M29B-Cosworth DFV	
dns	SOUTH AFRICAN GP	Kyalami	01/03/80	Marlboro Team McLaren	McLaren M29C-Cosworth DFV	*crash in practice/hurt wrist*
ret	BELGIAN GP	Zolder	04/05/80	Marlboro Team McLaren	McLaren M29C-Cosworth DFV	*transmission*
ret	MONACO GP	Monte Carlo	18/05/80	Marlboro Team McLaren	McLaren M29C-Cosworth DFV	*multiple accident*
ret	Spanish Grand Prix	Járama	01/06/80	Marlboro Team McLaren	McLaren M29C-Cosworth DFV	*engine/non-championship event*
ret	FRENCH GP	Paul Ricard	29/06/80	Marlboro Team McLaren	McLaren M29C-Cosworth DFV	*transmission*
6	BRITISH GP	Brands Hatch	13/07/80	Marlboro Team McLaren	McLaren M29C-Cosworth DFV	
11	GERMAN GP	Hockenheim	10/08/80	Marlboro Team McLaren	McLaren M29C-Cosworth DFV	*pit stop/skirt/tyre*
7	AUSTRIAN GP	Österreichring	17/08/80	Marlboro Team McLaren	McLaren M29C-Cosworth DFV	
6	DUTCH GP	Zandvoort	31/08/80	Marlboro Team McLaren	McLaren M30-Cosworth DFV	
7	ITALIAN GP	Imola	14/09/80	Marlboro Team McLaren	McLaren M30-Cosworth DFV	
ret	CANADIAN GP	Montreal	28/09/80	Marlboro Team McLaren	McLaren M30-Cosworth DFV	*suspension/accident*
dns	US GP EAST	Watkins Glen	05/10/80	Marlboro Team McLaren	McLaren M30-Cosworth DFV	*accident in practice/unwell*

1981

ret	US GP WEST	Long Beach	15/03/81	Equipe Renault Elf	Renault RE22B EF1	*hit by de Cesaris*
ret	BRAZILIAN GP	Rio	29/03/81	Equipe Renault Elf	Renault RE22B EF1	*hit by Pironi*
3	ARGENTINE GP	Buenos Aires	12/04/81	Equipe Renault Elf	Renault RE22B EF1	
ret	SAN MARINO GP	Imola	03/05/81	Equipe Renault Elf	Renault RE22B EF1	*gearbox*
ret	BELGIAN GP	Zolder	17/05/81	Equipe Renault Elf	Renault RE30 EF1	*clutch*
ret	MONACO GP	Monte Carlo	31/05/81	Equipe Renault Elf	Renault RE30 EF1	*engine*
ret	SPANISH GP	Járama	21/06/81	Equipe Renault Elf	Renault RE30 EF1	*spun off*
1	FRENCH GP	Dijon	05/07/81	Equipe Renault Elf	Renault RE30 EF1	*Fastest lap*
ret	BRITISH GP	Silverstone	18/07/81	Equipe Renault Elf	Renault RE30 EF1	*engine*
2	GERMAN GP	Hockenheim	02/08/81	Equipe Renault Elf	Renault RE30 EF1	*Pole*
ret	AUSTRIAN GP	Österreichring	16/08/81	Equipe Renault Elf	Renault RE30 EF1	*suspension*
1	DUTCH GP	Zandvoort	30/08/81	Equipe Renault Elf	Renault RE30 EF1	*Pole*
1	ITALIAN GP	Monza	13/09/81	Equipe Renault Elf	Renault RE30 EF1	
ret	CANADIAN GP	Montreal	27/09/81	Equipe Renault Elf	Renault RE30 EF1	*accident with Mansell*
2	CAESAR'S PALACE GP	Las Vegas	17/10/81	Equipe Renault Elf	Renault RE30 EF1	

1982

1	SOUTH AFRICAN GP	Kyalami	23/01/82	Equipe Renault Elf	Renault RE30B EF1	*Fastest lap*
1	BRAZILIAN GP	Rio	21/03/82	Equipe Renault Elf	Renault RE30B EF1	*Pole/1st + 2nd disqualified*
ret	US GP WEST	Long Beach	04/04/82	Equipe Renault Elf	Renault RE30B EF1	*accident/brakes*
ret	SAN MARINO GP	Imola	25/04/82	Equipe Renault Elf	Renault RE30B EF1	*engine*
ret	BELGIAN GP	Zolder	09/05/82	Equipe Renault Elf	Renault RE30B EF1	*spun off/Pole*
7/ret	MONACO GP	Monte Carlo	23/05/82	Equipe Renault Elf	Renault RE30B EF1	*spun off*
nc	US GP (DETROIT)	Detroit	06/06/82	Equipe Renault Elf	Renault RE30B EF1	*injector pump/Pole/Fastest lap*
ret	CANADIAN GP	Montreal	13/06/82	Equipe Renault Elf	Renault RE30B EF1	*engine*
ret	DUTCH GP	Zandvoort	03/07/82	Equipe Renault Elf	Renault RE30B EF1	*engine*
6	BRITISH GP	Brands Hatch	18/07/82	Equipe Renault Elf	Renault RE30B EF1	
2	FRENCH GP	Paul Ricard	25/07/82	Equipe Renault Elf	Renault RE30B EF1	
ret	GERMAN GP	Hockenheim	08/08/82	Equipe Renault Elf	Renault RE30B EF1	*fuel injection*
8/ret	AUSTRIAN GP	Österreichring	15/08/82	Equipe Renault Elf	Renault RE30B EF1	*fuel injection*
2	SWISS GP	Dijon	29/08/82	Equipe Renault Elf	Renault RE30B EF1	*Pole/Fastest lap*
ret	ITALIAN GP	Monza	12/09/82	Equipe Renault Elf	Renault RE30B EF1	*fuel injection*
4	CAESAR'S PALACE GP	Las Vegas	25/09/82	Equipe Renault Elf	Renault RE30B EF1	*Pole*
1	Australian GP	Calder	07/11/82	Calder Raceway	Ralt RT4-Ford BDA	*Pole*

1983

7	BRAZILIAN GP	Rio	13/03/83	Equipe Renault Elf	Renault RE30C EF1	
11	US GP WEST	Long Beach	27/03/83	Equipe Renault Elf	Renault RE40 EF1	*pit stop/misfire*
1	FRENCH GP	Paul Ricard	17/04/83	Equipe Renault Elf	Renault RE40 EF1	*Pole/Fastest lap*
2	SAN MARINO GP	Imola	01/05/83	Equipe Renault Elf	Renault RE40 EF1	
3	MONACO GP	Monte Carlo	15/05/83	Equipe Renault Elf	Renault RE40 EF1	*pit stop/tyres*
1	BELGIAN GP	Spa	22/05/83	Equipe Renault Elf	Renault RE40 EF1	*Pole*
8	US GP (DETROIT)	Detroit	05/06/83	Equipe Renault Elf	Renault RE40 EF1	*pit stop/tyres/fuel*
5	CANADIAN GP	Montreal	12/06/83	Equipe Renault Elf	Renault RE40 EF1	*pit stop/tyres/fuel*
1	BRITISH GP	Silverstone	16/07/83	Equipe Renault Elf	Renault RE40 EF1	*Fastest lap*
4	GERMAN GP	Hockenheim	07/08/83	Equipe Renault Elf	Renault RE40 EF1	*pit stop/tyres/fuel*
1	AUSTRIAN GP	Österreichring	14/08/83	Equipe Renault Elf	Renault RE40 EF1	*Fastest lap*
ret	DUTCH GP	Zandvoort	28/08/83	Equipe Renault Elf	Renault RE40 EF1	*collision with Piquet*
ret	ITALIAN GP	Monza	11/09/83	Equipe Renault Elf	Renault RE40 EF1	*turbo*
2	EUROPEAN GP	Brands Hatch	25/09/83	Equipe Renault Elf	Renault RE40 EF1	*pit stop/tyres/fuel*
ret	SOUTH AFRICAN GP	Kyalami	15/10/83	Equipe Renault Elf	Renault RE40 EF1	*turbo*

1984

1	BRAZILIAN GP	Rio	25/03/84	Marlboro McLaren	McLaren MP4/2-TAG PO1	*Fastest lap*
2	SOUTH AFRICAN GP	Kyalami	07/04/84	Marlboro McLaren	McLaren MP4/2-TAG PO1	*started from pit lane*
ret	BELGIAN GP	Zolder	29/04/84	Marlboro McLaren	McLaren MP4/2-TAG PO1	*distributor*
1	SAN MARINO GP	Imola	06/05/84	Marlboro McLaren	McLaren MP4/2-TAG PO1	
15	Inaugural Saloon Car Race	Nürburgring	12/05/84	Daimler Benz AG	Mercedes Benz 190E	
7	FRENCH GP	Dijon	20/05/84	Marlboro McLaren	McLaren MP4/2-TAG PO1	*2 pit stops/wheel/Fastest lap*
1	MONACO GP	Monte Carlo	03/06/84	Marlboro McLaren	McLaren MP4/2-TAG PO1	*race stopped/rain/Pole*
3	CANADIAN GP	Montreal	17/06/84	Marlboro McLaren	McLaren MP4/2-TAG PO1	*misfire*
5	US GP (DETROIT)	Detroit	24/06/84	Marlboro McLaren	McLaren MP4/2-TAG PO1	*2 pit stops/tyres*
ret	US GP (DALLAS)	Dallas	08/07/84	Marlboro McLaren	McLaren MP4/2-TAG PO1	*hit wall*
ret	BRITISH GP	Brands Hatch	22/07/84	Marlboro McLaren	McLaren MP4/2-TAG PO1	*gearbox*
1	GERMAN GP	Hockenheim	05/08/84	Marlboro McLaren	McLaren MP4/2-TAG PO1	*Pole/Fastest lap*
ret	AUSTRIAN GP	Österreichring	19/08/84	Marlboro McLaren	McLaren MP4/2-TAG PO1	*spun off*
1	DUTCH GP	Zandvoort	26/08/84	Marlboro McLaren	McLaren MP4/2-TAG PO1	*Pole*
ret	ITALIAN GP	Monza	09/09/84	Marlboro McLaren	McLaren MP4/2-TAG PO1	*engine*
1	EUROPEAN GP	Nürburgring	07/10/84	Marlboro McLaren	McLaren MP4/2-TAG PO1	
1	PORTUGUESE GP	Estoril	21/10/84	Marlboro McLaren	McLaren MP4/2-TAG PO1	

1985

1	BRAZILIAN GP	Rio	07/04/85	Marlboro McLaren	McLaren MP4/2B-TAG PO1	*Fastest lap*
ret	PORTUGUESE GP	Estoril	21/04/85	Marlboro McLaren	McLaren MP4/2B-TAG PO1	*spun off*
dsq	SAN MARINO GP	Imola	05/05/85	Marlboro McLaren	McLaren MP4/2B-TAG PO1	*1st on road/under weight limit*
1	MONACO GP	Monte Carlo	19/05/85	Marlboro McLaren	McLaren MP4/2B-TAG PO1	
3	CANADIAN GP	Montreal	16/06/85	Marlboro McLaren	McLaren MP4/2B-TAG PO1	
ret	US GP (DETROIT)	Detroit	23/06/85	Marlboro McLaren	McLaren MP4/2B-TAG PO1	*accident/brakes*
3	FRENCH GP	Paul Ricard	07/07/85	Marlboro McLaren	McLaren MP4/2B-TAG PO1	
1	BRITISH GP	Silverstone	21/07/85	Marlboro McLaren	McLaren MP4/2B-TAG PO1	*Fastest lap*
2	GERMAN GP	Nürburgring	04/08/85	Marlboro McLaren	McLaren MP4/2B-TAG PO1	
1	AUSTRIAN GP	Österreichring	18/08/85	Marlboro McLaren	McLaren MP4/2B-TAG PO1	*Pole/Fastest lap*
2	DUTCH GP	Zandvoort	25/08/85	Marlboro McLaren	McLaren MP4/2B-TAG PO1	*Fastest lap*
1	ITALIAN GP	Monza	08/09/85	Marlboro McLaren	McLaren MP4/2B-TAG PO1	
3	BELGIAN GP	Spa	15/09/85	Marlboro McLaren	McLaren MP4/2B-TAG PO1	*Pole/Fastest lap*
4	EUROPEAN GP	Brands Hatch	06/10/85	Marlboro McLaren	McLaren MP4/2B-TAG PO1	
3	SOUTH AFRICAN GP	Kyalami	19/10/85	Marlboro McLaren	McLaren MP4/2B-TAG PO1	
ret	AUSTRALIAN GP	Adelaide	03/11/85	Marlboro McLaren	McLaren MP4/2B-TAG PO1	*engine*

1986

ret	BRAZILIAN GP	Rio	23/03/86	Marlboro McLaren	McLaren MP4/2C-TAG PO1	*engine*
3	SPANISH GP	Jerez	13/04/86	Marlboro McLaren	McLaren MP4/2C-TAG PO1	
1	SAN MARINO GP	Imola	27/04/86	Marlboro McLaren	McLaren MP4/2C-TAG PO1	
1	MONACO GP	Monte Carlo	11/05/86	Marlboro McLaren	McLaren MP4/2C-TAG PO1	*Pole/Fastest lap*
6	BELGIAN GP	Spa	25/05/86	Marlboro McLaren	McLaren MP4/2C-TAG PO1	*pit stop/nose/Fastest lap*
2	CANADIAN GP	Montreal	15/06/86	Marlboro McLaren	McLaren MP4/2C-TAG PO1	
3	US GP (DETROIT)	Detroit	22/06/86	Marlboro McLaren	McLaren MP4/2C-TAG PO1	
2	FRENCH GP	Paul Ricard	06/07/86	Marlboro McLaren	McLaren MP4/2C-TAG PO1	
3	BRITISH GP	Brands Hatch	13/07/86	Marlboro McLaren	McLaren MP4/2C-TAG PO1	
6	GERMAN GP	Hockenheim	27/07/86	Marlboro McLaren	McLaren MP4/2C-TAG PO1	
ret	HUNGARIAN GP	Hungaroring	10/08/86	Marlboro McLaren	McLaren MP4/2C-TAG PO1	*accident with Arnoux*
1	AUSTRIAN GP	Österreichring	17/08/86	Marlboro McLaren	McLaren MP4/2C-TAG PO1	
dsq	ITALIAN GP	Monza	07/09/86	Marlboro McLaren	McLaren MP4/2C-TAG PO1	*changed cars after warm-up lap*
2	PORTUGUESE GP	Estoril	21/09/86	Marlboro McLaren	McLaren MP4/2C-TAG PO1	
2	MEXICAN GP	Mexico City	12/10/86	Marlboro McLaren	McLaren MP4/2C-TAG PO1	
1	AUSTRALIAN GP	Adelaide	26/10/86	Marlboro McLaren	McLaren MP4/2C-TAG PO1	

1987

1	BRAZILIAN GP	Rio	12/04/87	Marlboro McLaren	McLaren MP4/3-TAG PO1	
ret	SAN MARINO GP	Imola	03/05/87	Marlboro McLaren	McLaren MP4/3-TAG PO1	*alternator*
1	BELGIAN GP	Spa	17/05/87	Marlboro McLaren	McLaren MP4/3-TAG PO1	*Fastest lap*
9/ret	MONACO GP	Monte Carlo	31/05/87	Marlboro McLaren	McLaren MP4/3-TAG PO1	*engine*
3	US GP (DETROIT)	Detroit	21/06/87	Marlboro McLaren	McLaren MP4/3-TAG PO1	
3	FRENCH GP	Paul Ricard	05/07/87	Marlboro McLaren	McLaren MP4/3-TAG PO1	
ret	BRITISH GP	Silverstone	12/07/87	Marlboro McLaren	McLaren MP4/3-TAG PO1	*clutch/electrics*
7/ret	GERMAN GP	Hockenheim	26/07/87	Marlboro McLaren	McLaren MP4/3-TAG PO1	*alternator belt*
3	HUNGARIAN GP	Hungaroring	09/08/87	Marlboro McLaren	McLaren MP4/3-TAG PO1	
6	AUSTRIAN GP	Österreichring	16/08/87	Marlboro McLaren	McLaren MP4/3-TAG PO1	
15	ITALIAN GP	Monza	06/09/87	Marlboro McLaren	McLaren MP4/3-TAG PO1	*pit stop/misfire*
1	PORTUGUESE GP	Estoril	20/09/87	Marlboro McLaren	McLaren MP4/3-TAG PO1	
2	SPANISH GP	Jerez	27/09/87	Marlboro McLaren	McLaren MP4/3-TAG PO1	
ret	MEXICAN GP	Mexico City	18/10/87	Marlboro McLaren	McLaren MP4/3-TAG PO1	*accident with Piquet*
7	JAPANESE GP	Suzuka	01/11/87	Marlboro McLaren	McLaren MP4/3-TAG PO1	*pit stop/tyre/Fastest lap*
ret	AUSTRALIAN GP	Adelaide	15/11/87	Marlboro McLaren	McLaren MP4/3-TAG PO1	*brakes*

1988

1	BRAZILIAN GP	Rio	03/04/88	Honda Marlboro McLaren	McLaren MP4/4-Honda RA 168-E	
2	SAN MARINO GP	Imola	01/05/88	Honda Marlboro McLaren	McLaren MP4/4-Honda RA 168-E	*Fastest lap*
1	MONACO GP	Monte Carlo	15/05/88	Honda Marlboro McLaren	McLaren MP4/4-Honda RA 168-E	
1	MEXICAN GP	Mexico City	29/05/88	Honda Marlboro McLaren	McLaren MP4/4-Honda RA 168-E	*Fastest lap*
2	CANADIAN GP	Montreal	12/06/88	Honda Marlboro McLaren	McLaren MP4/4-Honda RA 168-E	
2	US GP (DETROIT)	Detroit	19/06/88	Honda Marlboro McLaren	McLaren MP4/4-Honda RA 168-E	*Fastest lap*
1	FRENCH GP	Paul Ricard	03/07/88	Honda Marlboro McLaren	McLaren MP4/4-Honda RA 168-E	*Pole/Fastest lap*
ret	BRITISH GP	Silverstone	10/07/88	Honda Marlboro McLaren	McLaren MP4/4-Honda RA 168-E	*handling*
2	GERMAN GP	Hockenheim	24/07/88	Honda Marlboro McLaren	McLaren MP4/4-Honda RA 168-E	
2	HUNGARIAN GP	Hungaroring	07/08/88	Honda Marlboro McLaren	McLaren MP4/4-Honda RA 168-E	*Fastest lap*
2	BELGIAN GP	Spa	28/08/88	Honda Marlboro McLaren	McLaren MP4/4-Honda RA 168-E	
ret	ITALIAN GP	Monza	11/09/88	Honda Marlboro McLaren	McLaren MP4/4-Honda RA 168-E	*engine*
1	PORTUGUESE GP	Estoril	25/09/88	Honda Marlboro McLaren	McLaren MP4/4-Honda RA 168-E	*Pole*
1	SPANISH GP	Jerez	02/10/88	Honda Marlboro McLaren	McLaren MP4/4-Honda RA 168-E	*Fastest lap*
2	JAPANESE GP	Suzuka	30/10/88	Honda Marlboro McLaren	McLaren MP4/4-Honda RA 168-E	
1	AUSTRALIAN GP	Adelaide	13/11/88	Honda Marlboro McLaren	McLaren MP4/4-Honda RA 168-E	*Fastest lap*

1989

2	BRAZILIAN GP	Rio	26/03/89	Honda Marlboro McLaren	McLaren MP4/5-Honda RA 109E	
2	SAN MARINO GP	Imola	23/04/89	Honda Marlboro McLaren	McLaren MP4/5-Honda RA 109E	*Fastest lap*
2	MONACO GP	Monte Carlo	07/05/89	Honda Marlboro McLaren	McLaren MP4/5-Honda RA 109E	*Fastest lap*
5	MEXICAN GP	Mexico City	28/05/89	Honda Marlboro McLaren	McLaren MP4/5-Honda RA 109E	*pit stop/tyres*
1	US GP (PHOENIX)	Phoenix	04/06/89	Honda Marlboro McLaren	McLaren MP4/5-Honda RA 109E	
ret	CANADIAN GP	Montreal	18/06/89	Honda Marlboro McLaren	McLaren MP4/5-Honda RA 109E	*suspension/Pole*
1	FRENCH GP	Paul Ricard	09/07/89	Honda Marlboro McLaren	McLaren MP4/5-Honda RA 109E	*Pole*
1	BRITISH GP	Silverstone	16/07/89	Honda Marlboro McLaren	McLaren MP4/5-Honda RA 109E	
2	GERMAN GP	Hockenheim	30/07/89	Honda Marlboro McLaren	McLaren MP4/5-Honda RA 109E	*gearbox problems when 1st*
4	HUNGARIAN GP	Hungaroring	13/08/89	Honda Marlboro McLaren	McLaren MP4/5-Honda RA 109E	*pit stop/tyres*
2	BELGIAN GP	Spa	27/08/89	Honda Marlboro McLaren	McLaren MP4/5-Honda RA 109E	*Fastest lap*
1	ITALIAN GP	Monza	10/09/89	Honda Marlboro McLaren	McLaren MP4/5-Honda RA 109E	*Fastest lap*
2	PORTUGUESE GP	Estoril	24/09/89	Honda Marlboro McLaren	McLaren MP4/5-Honda RA 109E	
3	SPANISH GP	Jerez	01/10/89	Honda Marlboro McLaren	McLaren MP4/5-Honda RA 109E	*gearbox problems*
ret	JAPANESE GP	Suzuka	22/10/89	Honda Marlboro McLaren	McLaren MP4/5-Honda RA 109E	*collision Senna/Fastest lap*
ret/dns	AUSTRALIAN GP	Adelaide	05/11/89	Honda Marlboro McLaren	McLaren MP4/5-Honda RA 109E	*protest/dangerous conditions*

**Formula 1 World Championship
positions/ points (1980-89)**

1980	14th	5
1981	5th	43
1982	4th	34
1983	2nd	57
1984	2nd	71.5
1985	1st	76
1986	1st	74
1987	4th	46
1988	2nd	105
1989	1st	81
		592.5

**Formula 1 World Championship placings 1st – 6th + Pole + Fastest laps
(1980-89)**

1st	*2nd*	*3rd*	*4th*	*5th*	*6th*	*Pole*	*Fastest lap*
39	27	14	5	3	7	20	31

Note:
Alain Prost raced karts prior to the commencement of his car racing career, winning
French and European championships during 1973-75. In 1975 he won the Pilote Elf
award at the Renault-Elf Winfield School at the Paul Ricard circuit, which enabled him
to compete in Formula Renault in 1976.